Where in the World Is God?

Harold L. Senkbeil

Devotions compiled by Beverly K. Yahnke

Northwestern
Publishing House
Milwaukee, Wisconsin

www.nph.net

Second printing, 2002

Library of Congress Card 98-66825
Northwestern Publishing House
1250 N. 113th St., Milwaukee, WI 53226-3284
© 1999 by Northwestern Publishing House
Published 1999
Printed in the United States of America
ISBN 0-8100-0897-1

To all who hear and do the Word
at
Elm Grove Ev. Lutheran Church
Elm Grove, Wisconsin

**To him who is able to keep you from falling
and to present you before his glorious presence
without fault and with great joy—
to the only God our Savior
be glory, majesty, power and authority,
through Jesus Christ our Lord,
before all ages,
now and forevermore! Amen.**

(Jude 24,25)

About these meditations—

As the twentieth century draws to a close and the dawning of a new millennium is upon us, Christians face a future bright with promise, yet darkened by uncertainty and fear. In this time of frenzied change, the church is called to faithfulness to her Lord and his unchanging Word. Those called to the preaching office in our day face a task humanly impossible— to proclaim the unsearchable riches of Christ in an increasingly jaded world to an increasingly uneasy church. But with God all things are possible. For 27 years now he has been teaching me the two-pronged art of preaching: faithfulness to his Word and sensitivity to his flock.

This book represents a distillation of some of my sermons in devotional form. Dr. Beverly Yahnke, parishioner and Christian psychologist, first outlined the project and guided it to completion, suggesting that these sermons may be helpful to Christians searching for hope and healing in the rubble of their lives. It is my hope and fervent prayer that some of the words which follow may be helpful for those who preach in the church and those who hear as well, that we all may capture anew the living voice of the gospel for our chaotic times.

Luther once supposedly advised that preachers pray the "Our Father" on the way up into the pulpit, but not coming down. By this he meant to say that the preacher should humbly seek forgiveness for his human preparation before the sermon, but afterwards boldly leave the results to God.

As long as sermon manuscripts remain filed safely away in obscurity, such faith is comparatively easy. When Dr. Yahnke suggested the present project, however, I was faced with weighing my words again according to the Word of God. My thanks to her for wading through my sermons to reduce them to devotional readings; much chaff had to be discarded. In sorting through such wheat as still remains, I pray once more that what belongs to my human weakness may be forgotten—so that those words that serve faithfully to echo the eternal Word of God may linger in your ear and on your heart.

Rev. Harold L. Senkbeil, STM
First Sunday in Advent
30 November, 1998

Contents

1. Backwards and Upside Down

Blessed are you when men hate you, when they exclude you and insult you and reject your name as evil, because of the Son of Man. Woe to you when all men speak well of you, for that is how their fathers treated the false prophets. (Luke 6:22,26)

It's clear that Jesus never took a Dale Carnegie course. By accepted standards he didn't know much about how to win friends and influence people. He probably wouldn't have been a very appealing after-dinner speaker either. Provocative he was; entertaining he was not. For there's nothing entertaining about the kingdom of God. Satisfying? Yes! Life-giving? Yes! But entertaining? No. Jesus did not come to make us feel good. He came to make us over again, into something entirely new.

Ordinary thinking cannot grasp what Jesus is preaching here. It seems backwards and upside down to us, but that's just the point. Our lives must be turned upside down if we are to be saved. In our world the rich are blessed, and the poor are pitied. Jesus goes to the innermost sanctum of our hearts. "What's most important to you?" he asks. "Is your heart fixed on the possessions of this world or on God himself?" If the most important things in life are our glorious God and the gracious gifts he gives us—the forgiveness of our sins for the sake of Jesus Christ, the life and the salvation he brings—then we have a grip on life that endures to all eternity. "Blessed are the poor," says Jesus, and he means you.

Our world is upside down, you see. Death has gained the upper hand. In Adam, all have died. But in Jesus Christ, life is restored, and God sets us right again. So you are not to fear or be dismayed as a Christian. Should you sense some emptiness and longing deep inside, God is beginning to turn you right side up. It is a sign of grace. Blessed are those who hunger, for those who hunger will be satisfied now with the good things of God's own house. Do not be dismayed if your hearts are gripped with sorrow; those tears of yours are good. Those who weep are blessed if they belong to Christ. Do not be surprised if life isn't always rosy. "Blessed are you when men hate you," Jesus says. It's a bad sign if everybody always speaks well of you in this world of sin. False prophets are always popular, but God's true servants are not.

When you live, act, and speak as a child of God through faith in Jesus Christ, you will be swimming against the stream; you may not always be admired. Sometimes people will mock you and insult you. But remember, God works in ways upside down and backwards; in heaven things will be right side up again. Until then we wait, confident and full of hope, trusting the Word preached in Jesus' name, being fed with his life-giving body and blood. We believe what we cannot see with our eyes. And believing, we rejoice.

Thanks be to you, my Lord Jesus Christ, for all the benefits you have won for me, for all the pains and insults you have borne for me. Most merciful Redeemer, friend, and brother, may I know you more clearly, love you more dearly, and follow you more nearly, for ever and ever. Amen.

Richard of Chichester

2. Bad Things and Good People

Do you think that these Galileans were worse sinners than all the other Galileans because they suffered this way? I tell you, no! But unless you repent, you too will all perish. (Luke 13:2,3)

If there's anything in life that turns us all into philosophers, it is the age-old problem of evil. If God is good, why is there evil? What can a good and gracious God intend by allowing calamities to fall upon his children? We can understand why the bad guys get theirs, but when tragedy strikes the good and upright, we get a bit uptight. "Why can't God be fair?" we wonder. "Where is the justice in this?" You know the questions; they pop up whenever the plot thickens in anyone's life: "Why did my mother have to die? Why did I lose my job? Why did my spouse leave me?" The people in the text had the same sort of questions. "Why did Pilate kill the Galileans while they were worshiping in God's temple?"

We keep thinking that we ought to be rewarded for good behavior and punished for bad behavior. Only bad people ought to suffer. But that's not the way it works in the kingdom of God. If you want to see how God operates, just take a look at the cross. There God meted out the just penalty for sin. But he punished the wrong guy! Jesus Christ, God's Son, was without sin. He had done nothing wrong. But there God balanced the scale of justice. All the weight of all the sins of all the people in all the world was placed on him. The weight of that guilt killed him. The only innocent man who ever lived was offered as the stand-in victim for the sins of the whole world. Bad things happened to a good man. In the death and resurrection of Jesus

Christ, the good things of God were passed on to all the bad people of the world.

"Unless you repent," says Jesus, "you too will all perish." Now that's pretty straight talk. In our world we measure worth and status by our accomplishments. So it's only natural that we carry that attitude over to our relationship with God. We think that what matters is that we're above average, and we have the idea that God must be fairly well-satisfied with us. Yet each of us, in his or her own way, stands guilty before God. Despite our good reputations and the admiration of our peers, we are all as guilty as sin. We stand condemned by the evil things we have done and by the good things we have left undone.

Thanks be to God that there is only one thing that really matters: Jesus Christ and his cross—his redeeming blood, shed for us. The forgiveness of sins, life, and salvation earned for us long ago are conveyed in the washing of his Baptism, in the eating of his Holy Supper, and in the word of his gospel absolution. Despite the evil in our world, "there is now no condemnation for those who are in Christ Jesus" (Romans 8:1). It's not fair! It's grace. This is God's own solution to the problem of evil.

O Lord Jesus Christ, as you discipline those you love: grant us grace, we pray, to see your love in whatever suffering you send us; support us in patient thankfulness under pain, anxiety, or loss; and move us with pity and tenderness for our suffering neighbors; for your mercy's sake. Amen.

Christina Rossetti

3. Bankrupt before God

The Spirit of the Sovereign LORD is on me, because the LORD has anointed me to preach good news to the poor. (Isaiah 61:1)

The poor: that's us! We're the spiritually poor, you and I. No matter what chunk of real estate we call our own, no matter what our earned income or list of assets, we are the ones who are poor before God— bankrupt is more like it. That's tough to take; it knocks all the props out from under us, you see. It means I have nothing to contribute to my salvation. Since God did it all, since he died in my place to bring me his love and his life, then I have nothing to bring to him. That means there's only one way to come to God—with empty hands, and in lowliness and weakness. Unsettling, isn't it?

You'd better believe it. There's nothing more humiliating than lowliness and weakness for people like us. Hard workers and self-starters that we are, nothing is further from our minds than this kind of weakness and emptiness. And we would rather die than come to God with empty hands. After all, we're not all that bad, or so we'd like to think. We live upstanding lives. We're church people, for crying out loud. We try our level best. Well, we try at least as hard as anyone else does to live the Christian life. You mean we're going to have to lay all that aside and come to God with nothing? We would rather die.

And that's exactly it. Our sinful pride does have to die. That's the whole thing about the grace and mercy of God. It is so completely all-inclusive that there's no room for anything else, including our own measly efforts toward our own salvation. All our pious talk and our nice religiosity don't hide a thing. The fact that we hang around church a lot won't change anything.

What changes things is Christ. For through his poverty we become rich. Jesus our Lord left all the glory of heaven, set aside all his majesty as God to lower himself and become one of us, in lowliness and weakness, to share in our poverty. Not only did he take on our human flesh, but he also came here to die our death, to bear all our sin in his own body. That means that every last person baptized into him has a share in the wealth of his assets. The forgiveness of sin, the life, and the salvation that are his alone, he credits to our account. The assets of Jesus are more than enough to cover the spiritual liabilities of us all, no matter who we are. We come to God in utter poverty, and we have nothing to lose except our sin. What a privilege to have the good news preached to us in Christ's church, to be in his presence, and to receive the abundance of his lavish gifts. The life of Christ in exchange for the death of our sin: Good news for the poor, indeed!

Lord, as you have called us, you have called us to open our hands so that you might fill them, but our sinful hands resist. Open not only our hands, but our hearts also, so that we may know nothing but you, count all things loss in comparison with you, and desire to be made like you. Through Jesus Christ our Lord. Amen.

Jeremy Taylor

4. Baptized into Christ

For as many of you as have been baptized into Christ have put on Christ. (Galatians 3:27 KJV)

This is a verse familiar to many of us; yet if we are honest we might admit that we're not entirely sure what it means for us as we go about the challenge of living day to day. Just what does it mean to be "baptized into Christ" and to "put on Christ"?

We can learn from our children playing "dress up." When children put on someone else's clothing, their actions and vocabulary change. They become that person. So it is with all the baptized faithful. In Baptism we "have put on Christ," that is, we are so intimately linked with the Lord Jesus that all we are becomes his and all he is becomes ours. Goodness, kindness, meekness, and gentleness belong to none of us by nature. These are the qualities of Jesus. But being clothed with Jesus by Baptism, you see, all these qualities become ours as well. These are the very real gifts that belong to every baptized believer.

A glorious hymn, written nearly three hundred years ago, captures the power of Baptism with its repeated, joyful refrain: I am baptized into Christ. This conviction is the great sword with which we do battle against the evil one. This sweet promise comforts us in every time of trial. This proud confession is the sure confidence by which we live and, by the grace of God, in which we shall die. Being baptized into Christ, we shall stand by faith before the judgment seat of God, clothed not in our sin but in the glorious robes of the very righteousness and holiness of our dear Lord Jesus Christ.

Reassuring, isn't it? Time and again, despite our best intentions, we find ourselves caving in to the dictates of our sinful nature. Setting out to do the right thing, we do the wrong thing. Try as we might, we cannot rid ourselves of evil. The imagination of our hearts gets the better of us. And the lust of the flesh and the lust of the eyes and the pride of life takes over. Desire gives birth to sin. And sin, when it is full-grown, brings forth death. What wretched people we are by nature. But thanks be to God, through Jesus Christ our Lord! Since we are baptized into Christ, we have already died to sin; we stand forgiven and restored. As the devil has no power over Christ, so shall he have no power over us.

"I am baptized into Christ." This is our lifelong confidence, our fearless testimony before the ungodly of this world and before the very hordes of hell itself. By the grace of God, this shall be the sum of the faith in which we die: I am baptized into Christ.

Now my life is new and holy; I am baptized into Christ. Clothed in him, I live within him, and he is alive in me. For the sin and death I carried, now within his grave lies buried . Since by grace I'm dead to sin, now by grace I live in him. Amen.

Harold L. Senkbeil

5. Before Time Began

Blessed be the God and Father of our Lord Jesus Christ, who has blessed us in Christ with every spiritual blessing in the heavenly places, even as he chose us in him before the foundation of the world, that we should be holy and blameless before him. (Ephesians 1:3,4 RSV)

The sands of time keep slipping through the hourglass of history, but the child of God has a foothold on something rooted in eternity. We live in this world but are not of it. We stand flat-footed on earth, but our citizenship is in heaven. That makes all the difference in the world. Others may fear what awaits in the next millennium. We face the future calmly because our identity in this world is based on God's action before the foundation of the world. Our heavenly Father has chosen us in Christ before time began, that we might serve him here in time. "He chose us in him before the foundation of the world, that we should be holy and blameless before him."

Although we know the choosing is his work alone, we reason that the holiness must be our work. That's the trouble: We keep thinking that salvation is God's department, but holy living is our department. No wonder things keep going sour in our department. For we have no holiness in this world apart from the holiness designed before the foundation of the world. The only holy life we have to live here in time began in eternity, when our heavenly Father chose us in his beloved Son, Jesus Christ, to be his own beloved children.

Already then he had designed the whole wonderful master plan, which includes not only the payment for our sin, but also the very lives we live here in this world as his children. Jesus Christ is not only our justification and redemption, the Bible says, but he is also our sanctification. The whole kit and caboodle—salvation and life; forgiveness and holy living, that is, faith and works—is all of one piece. What God our Father wants us to do, he equips us to do in his Son, Jesus Christ our Lord.

Not only has the Father redeemed us, he has also sanctified us. Not only has he made the payment for our sins, he has also given us a holy life to live. It is a holiness not of our own making. The Father planned our salvation so that we were redeemed with the holy, precious blood of his Son in such a way that we might live under him in his kingdom and serve him in everlasting righteousness, innocence, and blessedness. It's all of one piece—both faith and life, believing and doing, salvation and living. And it's all ours in Jesus Christ, wrapped up in one big, glorious package and delivered to us as a gift in his Holy Word and sacraments that we might receive it by faith. That's what his kingdom is all about. God's kingdom comes when our heavenly Father gives us his Holy Spirit so that by his grace we believe his Holy Word and thus lead godly lives here in time and there in eternity.

O God, our help in ages past,
Our hope for years to come,
Still be our guard while troubles last
And our eternal home! Amen.

Isaac Watts

6. The Best for Last

This, the first of his miraculous signs, Jesus performed in Cana of Galilee. He thus revealed his glory, and his disciples put their faith in him. (John 2:11)

Water into wine, and wine of the highest quality: it was a miracle. But when you come right down to it, this wasn't much of a miracle, as miracles go. Jesus certainly performed many other miracles that seem to have been more important. Running out of wine at a wedding party just doesn't seem to be the end of the world, after all. Yet there is comfort in the fact that Jesus chose to reveal his extraordinary power for the very first time in a very ordinary situation. There comes a time for each of us, after all, when the wine runs out. Our problems are not necessarily all earth-shaking events or matters of life and death. Once in a while, as we juggle all our responsibilities, life starts to unravel, and our neat little world starts coming unglued. Like the time the wine ran out in Cana.

Mary knew what to do. She went to her son. What he was going to do, she had no idea. But he would do something; she was absolutely convinced. I wonder if we have that kind of confidence, to bring our most common and ordinary frustrations and lay them before the Lord in utter simplicity. What do you do when the wine runs out in your life? Complain? Fret? Or do you turn to the One who can do something about it? Mary told the servants, "Do whatever he tells you." She knew Jesus well enough to know that whatever he commands is right. Whatever he says is true.

Still, how hard it is to do whatever Jesus tells us! When we come to him with our problems, we would

11

like to hear him say, "Have it your way." But instead, Jesus tells us to deny ourselves and take up our cross and follow him. Jesus tells us to repent and to believe the gospel, but we are so proud in our sin that we would rather believe only in ourselves. "Do whatever he tells you," Mary said. That's good advice for the servants at the wedding feast and good advice for us too: "Do whatever he tells you." Though it makes no sense to our natural mind, we believe his Holy Word. In the word of his absolution, in the washing of his Baptism, and in his Holy Supper, we receive his pardon and peace. There is life in that Word.

It's no different today than it was in Cana. Jesus speaks his Word. And we do whatever he tells us. Come what may; in thick or thin; for better, for worse; for richer, for poorer; in sickness and in health; he has pledged us his faithfulness. He will never part from us. His love surrounds us; his compassion supports us. Like the wine in Cana, his gift, his miracle, is the best. And he saves the best for last. On the Last Day, he will raise us all from our graves and give everyone who believes in him the life that has no end. And that will be the best of all!

Almighty God, as you have made us for yourself and our hearts are restless till they find their rest in you, teach us to rely on you in all our needs so that we may be at peace and finally see you face-to-face. Through Jesus Christ our Lord. Amen

Australian Anglican Alternative Collects, adapted

7. Blind Faith?

Though you have not seen him, you love him; and even though you do not see him now, you believe in him and are filled with an inexpressible and glorious joy. (1 Peter 1:8)

If seeing is believing, we are at a distinct disadvantage. Not one of us has ever seen Jesus with his eyes. Not one of us has ever explored the wound in the side of Jesus with his own hand or placed his finger in the marks left by the nails that tore Jesus' flesh. We have not seen, and yet we believe. How can this be?

There were a whole lot of people who saw Jesus in the flesh and yet did not believe in him. With God, seeing is one thing, and faith is another. What counts with God is faith. Whoever believes and is baptized shall not perish but have everlasting life. Without having seen Jesus, we love him. Is this blind faith? No, it's a miracle of God. God continues to work faith in all his children, renewing them by his Holy Spirit, burying them by Baptism with his own Son, and raising them up along with him to live a new life by faith, not by sight. By faith alone we receive God's many blessings.

The same Lord Jesus who stood among his disciples and said "Peace be with you" (Luke 24:36) shares that same blessing among us. The church, in her liturgy, extends Jesus' greeting to all believers. Whenever the pastor says, "The peace of the Lord be with you," he doesn't mean "Have a nice day." For by the command and promise of Jesus, whenever two or more are gathered in his name, the Lord Jesus himself is present with his peace. His living flesh and real blood are distributed in his Holy Supper for us Christians to eat and to drink.

His living Word is among us, read and preached, sung and prayed for our ears to hear and our hearts to believe. He extends his peace to us again and again—his peace, purchased by his holy, precious blood when he was crucified, died, and was buried and then raised for us. So, at his divine command and trusting in his promise, we receive with inexpressible and glorious joy what we cannot now see but yet believe: forgiveness of sins, life, and salvation.

No, we do not see him now. But we still believe, in spite of the fact that the winds of adversity may blow long and hard. Trials and tribulations may have us in their grip. Fear and affliction come our way, and sometimes we may suffer grief and pain. Yet we are not dismayed. For even gold must be refined in a fire. How much more so must our faith, which is far more precious than gold, be refined and purified by testing and trial. Yet we are not afraid because ours is no blind faith. Our Lord Jesus remains among us. Though we have not seen him, yet we love him. Therefore take to heart the Word of Jesus spoken for you, "Blessed are those who have not seen and yet have believed" (John 20:29).

Almighty Father, as you made the disciples glad by the sight of the risen Lord, give us such knowledge of his presence with us, that we may be sustained by his risen life and serve you continually in righteousness and truth. Through Jesus Christ our Lord. Amen.

Australian Anglican Alternative Collects, adapted

8. Born Again

Praise be to the God and Father of our Lord Jesus Christ! In his great mercy he has given us new birth into a living hope through the resurrection of Jesus Christ from the dead. (1 Peter 1:3)

People have always had a hard time understanding what it means to be born again. Some ignore it, considering it only a figure of speech. Others insist being born again is some kind of spiritual experience by which people consciously choose to accept Jesus by an act of their own will. Jesus, of course, explained exactly what he had in mind. This rebirth, he told Nicodemus, is a birth by water and the Spirit. In other words, it is the rebirth of Holy Baptism. This is the new birth we all need, for as Jesus explained, "I tell you the truth, no one can enter the kingdom of God unless he is born of water and the Spirit" (John 3:5). By water and the Spirit, our gracious God begets us new as his sons and daughters and brings us into his own family, with all the rights and privileges of his inheritance. By this wondrous bath, he works forgiveness of sins, rescues from death and the devil, and gives eternal salvation to all who believe.

So what difference does this new birth make? It makes a world of difference. By this rebirth the cross and resurrection of Jesus intersect with our lives. St. Paul writes, "We were therefore buried with him through baptism into death in order that, just as Christ was raised from the dead through the glory of the Father, we too may live a new life" (Romans 6:4).

New life, new hope. Now that's good news if there ever was any. How many times don't you and I find ourselves wishing we could start all over again? So often we struggle with remorse and guilt, the product of harsh words, bitter anger, or worse. The memory of that sin is almost too much to bear. It ought to be, because unrepented sin destroys us. If it's not the shame of past sin, it's the uncertain future that plagues us. We'd all like some guarantees about what days ahead may bring. Indeed, there are no promises that everything will work out fine in life and we'll have every-thing we've always hoped for. Still the hope continues— the living hope that is ours in the living Lord.

It is a living hope, thanks to the resurrection of Jesus Christ from the dead. And by Baptism we have been born again into this living hope. Baptism and faith, forgiveness of sin, life and salvation, they all go together. Because they do, we have hope in this hopeless world. Hope that is seen is not hope, of course. And so in order to increase our faith, God asks us to believe in the things we cannot see with our eyes. "Though you have not seen him, you love him; and even though you do not see him now, you believe in him and are filled with an inexpressible and glorious joy, for you are receiving the goal of your faith, the salvation of your souls" (1 Peter 1:8,9).

We pray, Lord, that we who have been adopted as your children by grace, being dead to sin, may live to right-eousness, and being buried with Christ in his death, may put to death our old self and destroy our sinful nature. Let us who share in the death of your Son share also in his resurrection. Through Jesus Christ our Lord. Amen.

Book of Common Prayer, 1549

9. The Call to Discipleship

"The time has come," he [Jesus] said. "The kingdom of God is near. Repent and believe the good news!" As Jesus walked beside the Sea of Galilee, he saw Simon and his brother Andrew. . . . "Come, follow me," Jesus said, "and I will make you fishers of men." (Mark 1:15-17)

If we are to understand the call to discipleship, it's important to keep in mind that there are two separate invitations given by our Lord in this text. The first is public—the gospel is always an invitation to faith. The second is personal—apprenticeship in the school of the apostles. The second invitation may seem more glamorous, but it rests on the first; the invitation to faith is the most important.

Fresh from his baptism, Jesus came proclaiming, "The kingdom of God is near." So he said, and so it was. For in his body all the fullness of God was pleased to dwell. When Jesus drew near, the kingdom of God drew near. Where he opened his mouth to speak, the good news of the kingdom came out. "Repent," he said, "and believe." Believe the good news. He that believes and is baptized shall be saved. This is our common calling in the church. This is the preaching that preceded the recruitment call to Simon and Andrew, to James and John. This is the preaching of the gospel, which awakened faith in them, and this is the preaching that brings forth faith among us as well.

Few are called to be public fishers of men—ministers of reconciliation as preachers or teachers of God's good news. But all of us are called to the good news of God and the forgiveness of our sins in Jesus' name. The Lord beckoned Simon and Andrew away from their nets and James and John away from their father's boat to train them as his ambassadors and representatives, fishers of men. But some fishermen he first called to faith and then sent back home.

We might welcome a call from our Lord that would summon us to leave behind our nets and follow him. It might be nice to abandon schedules, pressing work requirements, and our routine obligations in exchange for some exciting, globetrotting mission nearly anywhere else. Yet for most of us, the Lord's call to discipleship means faithfully tending the nets we've been given for now.

He calls each of us to be his own, whether fishers of men or fishers of fish! To each of us, the good news still comes. Repent, turn away from sin, and believe the good news: All you who are baptized into his death and life belong to him, and he will be your life this very day.

Remember, Lord, what you have worked in us and not what we deserve. As you have called us to your service, make us worthy of our calling through Jesus Christ our Lord. Amen.

Leonine

10. Called to Be Holy

Paul, called to be an apostle of Christ Jesus by the will of God, and our brother Sosthenes, To the church of God in Corinth, to those sanctified in Christ Jesus and called to be holy, together with all those everywhere who call on the name of our Lord Jesus Christ—their Lord and ours. (1 Corinthians 1:1,2)

"To the church of God in Corinth." The address sounds so pious that one would never have guessed Corinth was a hotbed of impurity. It was a city that put out the red carpet for people looking for overindulgence of every sort. So vile and so corrupt was the lifestyle of Corinth that the Greek world used the name of this city as a slang term for corruption. It would have seemed to be the last place on earth that God would have a church. If the church is, indeed, the bride of Christ, we're tempted to ask, "What's a nice girl like you doing in a place like *this?*"

Called to be holy. God's people are called to be holy in unholy places. That's the difficulty of leading a Christian life in a world that seems to be increasingly unchristian. How are we to be holy when the world we live in is so literally damned unholy? What else but damnable can you call the lifestyles so openly touted and advocated in our society? Homosexuals brazenly parade demands for what they call their "alternative lifestyle." In the name of personal privacy, women are given the right to take the lives of the unborn children they carry. And now, in the name of personal privacy, some clamor for the right to end their own lives. Such is the world we live in. We weep for our world, and we should, because it is lost and without hope without Christ.

But so are we. Without Christ we too would be lost and without hope. We condemn sin in the world around us. But have you every noticed how obvious and obnoxious the world's sin is, while our own sin remains quite hidden and, therefore, respectable? Such are the damnable lies of the devil. If he cannot lead us to despair because of our sin, he deceives us into believing we have no sin, or at least that our particular kind of sin is not as bad as the sins of others. So, being rightly shocked at the depraved world around us, we become quite blind to our own depravity.

We are called to be holy. Like the Corinthian Christians, we are washed, justified, and sanctified in the name of the Lord Jesus Christ by the Spirit of our God. Jesus Christ makes sinners into saints. Made holy by his precious blood, we are called to live in this depraved world, no longer making provision for our sinful nature, but instead living for the One who died for us and was raised again. Believing his Holy Word, we receive his holy body and precious blood upon our lips to purge away our guilt and bring us his divine life to live in righteousness and purity forever.

May God himself, the God of peace, sanctify you through and through. May your whole spirit, soul and body be kept blameless at the coming of our Lord Jesus Christ. Amen.

1 Thessalonians 5:23

11. Coming Out on Top

Sitting down, Jesus called the Twelve and said, "If anyone wants to be first, he must be the very last, and the servant of all." (Mark 9:35)

From the look of things in the world we live in, virtually everybody wants to be first! The whole idea is to get ahead. We are told that if you just wear the right jeans, drive the right car, and make the right income, you can come out on top. The idea is that if you want to be somebody, you'll have to make something of yourself; nobody else will do it for you. Blow your own horn and, by all means, do unto others before they do it to you. "Me First" could be the motto for our age. So it would seem that everybody would be interested in what Jesus has to say, "If anyone wants to be first . . .".

But it's the rest of what Jesus has to say that goes against our grain, ". . . he must be the very last, and the servant of all." Jesus didn't just talk about it; he did it. He came out on top in the end, but first he finished last in the world's eyes—dead last. That day at Calvary after Christ died, soldiers stuck a spear into his side and out came blood and water, the sign of death. But it was life for us—life in all its fullness for all who trust in him, instead of the death that comes naturally in this world. All for one reason: Jesus Christ was last of all and servant of all.

That's what continues in the church. Today the Lord Jesus goes on being the servant of all, serving us through the means of his grace. Here is our heavenly waiter, dishing up heaping helpings of the rich abundance of an eternal banquet that begins here and now in his church. Our servant Jesus serves up life out of death—life in the forgiveness of sins, the resurrection of the body, and the life everlasting through faith. He remains the servant of all in his holy church. Behind every sermon preached in his name, behind every Baptism done in his name, behind every Supper eaten in his name stands Jesus himself, dispensing his very life in our world of death.

In the final resurrection, it will be clear that this world has had it wrong all along. Sin, greed, power, and lust of all kinds seem to be the keys to success in our world; yet kindness, gentleness, peace, and patience are looked down upon as though they are for gutless, spineless people. Jesus teaches us that we live in an upside down world. The people at the bottom of the heap now—the ones who are servants of all for Jesus' sake—will end up at the top in the end. He was the last of all, but he is now the first of all. He came not to be served, but to serve. God has highly exalted him and given him the name above every name. At the name of Jesus, every knee should bow and every tongue confess that Jesus Christ is Lord to the glory of God the Father. When he returns there will be no choice.

Take out of our hearts, O Lord God, all self-assertion and boasting, all high and vain thoughts, all desire to excuse ourselves proudly with others, and grant us rather to take as master and king him who chose to be crowned with thorns and to die in shame for others and for us all, your Son, our Savior, Jesus Christ. Amen.

Charles John Vaughan

12. The Disturbing Peace of Christ

Do not suppose that I have come to bring peace to the earth. I did not come to bring peace, but a sword. (Matthew 10:34)

This doesn't sound like the Jesus we know, the Jesus who speaks of love and reconciliation. We know the kind, wise, gentle Savior who was always giving his familiar greeting: Peace be with you. And so we ask, Who is this Jesus, this Jesus who says he has not come to bring peace, but a sword? This Jesus we don't know much about. And that's a pity, because his message plants the gospel squarely in the midst of life, where people shoulder burdens, where the innocent sometimes suffer, where people hurt, and where people die. Jesus came to bring his peace right into the heart of this world of ours, and that can be disturbing.

The peace of Jesus Christ always comes across as a threat to the world, for his is a peace the world does not know. It surpasses the world's understanding. The peace of God comes to disturb our own little world, where a false god named Me, Myself, and I is enthroned as the king of the universe. The peace of Jesus Christ calls us out of that little world, topples the false god, casts us down from our seat as king of the world, and installs the rightful King instead. Christ's peace wars against sin.

The peace of Christ is a sword. It means the death of sin, even the sin that lies in our own hearts. We get all wrapped up in ourselves. Not only is that a miserable way to live, it's also a horrible way to die. Jesus spells that out very clearly, "Whoever finds his life will lose it, and whoever loses his life for my sake will find it" (Matthew 10:39). Jesus teaches that those who are locked up in their own little world, with themselves as their own god, will perish; but those who lay all that aside will find real life. Real life is something we can't grab for ourselves; we can only receive it as it is given under the cross of Jesus.

The cross was the sword Jesus used to demolish the grip of sin and death. We can understand why Jesus had to die on his cross, we just don't grasp why we should have to take up a cross in our own lives. Yet God often uses hardships to do his gracious work in our lives, teaching us more about his love and grace. When we shoulder the crosses of our lives, we meet the one who took up his cross that we might live. He is present in his Holy Word to strengthen us. He is present to nourish us in the Holy Supper of his body and blood, once given in payment for the sin of the world. We find that when we are weakest, that's when we are truly strong in the strength of his love. We learn that his grace is sufficient. His cross is disturbing only to sin and guilt and shame. By his cross Jesus brings us his life in all its abundance. Therefore, bearing our crosses gladly, we find out what that life is all about.

> **Then let us follow Christ our Lord**
> **And take the cross appointed.**
> **And, firmly clinging to his Word,**
> **In suff'ring be undaunted.**
> **For those who bear the battle's strain**
> **The crown of heav'nly life obtain. Amen.**

Johann Scheffler

13. Don't Cry

When the Lord saw her, his heart went out to her and he said, "Don't cry." (Luke 7:13)

"Don't cry." Two little words that come very easily to our lips when we see someone in tears. The incident from which this text was taken involved wounded souls and broken hearts. "Don't cry" seems a trifle inadequate.

Jesus and his disciples came up to the village of Nain just as a funeral procession was making its way out of the village gates. It was a sad scene. The dead person was a young man. Somehow, the death of a young person always seems especially tragic. He was the only son of his mother, and that intensified the tragedy. She was a widow. That seemed like the last straw. Now she was all alone in the world. She had no husband to support her, and her only son was dead. But then along came another only son—the only Son of God.

"When the Lord saw her," St. Luke records, "his heart went out to her." That's a rough translation. Actually, it was a more visceral reaction. Jesus felt the pain of this widow. He saw that she was left totally alone in this world and helpless in her grief. It hit him hard, and he felt for her. So Jesus said, "Don't cry." But what Jesus said was more than just these words. That's the point. For, when Jesus had said this, he reached out and touched the burial cot. "Young man," Jesus said to the corpse, "I say to you, get up!" And the dead man sat up and began to speak. Jesus returned him to his mother.

When Jesus walked into the life of this widow at Nain, God came to call. When God walks in on your life, things begin to change. And we could use a change. That's for sure! The tragedy is that too many of us are content to muddle along through life under our own power, without repentance, and living in open rebellion against God. And that's a crying shame.

Yet in his Holy Word and sacraments, Jesus reaches out to every sinner. We do not feel the touch of his hand, but he reaches out to touch us, nevertheless. Into our ears he places his Word, and into our mouths he places his very body and blood, once given and shed for the forgiveness of our sins. We don't see these things, to be sure, but we have his Word on it. In that Word there is healing and hope. Jesus says don't cry to broken and contrite hearts. When the Spirit works on our hearts through the Word, we find healing. Hearts are brave to hope again, and arms are strong to love and serve.

Almighty and eternal God, the comfort of the sad, the strength of those who suffer, let the prayers of your children who cry out in any trouble come before you, and to every soul who is distressed, grant mercy, grant relief, and grant refreshment through Jesus Christ our Lord. Amen.

Based on a Gregorian collect and Liturgy of St. Mark

14. Eating Humble Pie

Everyone who exalts himself will be humbled, and he who humbles himself will be exalted. (Luke 14:11)

At first reading, the advice seems to be straight from Miss Manners or some other advice columnist. "When someone invites you to a wedding feast, do not take the place of honor, for a person more distinguished than you may have been invited" (Luke 14:8). But this is not just protocol for formal affairs in ancient times. Rather, our Lord Jesus teaches us an important lesson about the kingdom of God. He teaches humility.

Now here's a lesson we all need to learn, for humility does not come naturally to the likes of us. Given the choice, we usually pick the driver's seat rather than the back seat. That's the way we run our cars, and that's the way we run our lives. There's something in us that doesn't take kindly to humility. That something in us, of course, is sin, and there's nothing new about that. Sinful pride has been around ever since Adam chose self-esteem over God's Word and thereby brought sin and death into the world. Pride is nothing new, but sinful pride seems to be on the increase. Self-esteem is in and humility is out. Self-assertion is the name of the game. Exalt yourself and you win. Humble yourself and you lose.

We manage to keep things under control much of the time. But that ugly, sinful pride is just beneath the surface all the while. When no one recognizes our hard work or someone else gets the glory we think we deserve, something snaps inside. That pride of ours is unleashed. Then look out, because there's hell to pay. Our God has a word for such pride. And it's a word of judgment: "For all that is in the world, the lust of the flesh, and the lust of the eyes, and the pride of life, is not of the Father, but is of the world. And the world passeth away, and the lust thereof" (1 John 2:16,17 KJV). The end result of pride is the sure and certain judgment of God. There IS hell to pay.

Fortunately, Jesus has shown us what true humility is all about. When he was reviled, he did not revile in return. When he suffered, he did not threaten. By his death on the cross, he has given us a new life to live—a life marked not by pride but by humility. For everyone baptized into his death bears the sign of the cross. And by his cross we live.

We find in Jesus not just some great example of humility, but our very life. No one else in all the world could carry our sin or bear our sorrow as he has done. No one else can put together the shattered pieces of our lives and make them whole again. We cannot take back the hurtful, spiteful words we've said or the ache and the pain we have caused by our proud actions. But Jesus can. In his forgiveness he wipes them all away and makes us clean and new. He sets us free to live again.

> **When I survey the wondrous cross**
> **On which the Prince of glory died,**
> **My richest gain I count but loss**
> **And pour contempt on all my pride. Amen.**

Isaac Watts

15. A Feast in the Wilderness

Moses and Aaron, Nadab and Abihu, and the seventy
elders of Israel went up and saw the God of Israel.
Under his feet was something like a pavement made of
sapphire, clear as the sky itself. But God did not raise
his hand against these leaders of the Israelites; they
saw God, and they ate and drank. (Exodus 24:9-11)

There's something a little alarming about this Old
Testament passage. Usually the Scriptures are very
comforting. So why, we ask, would God "raise his
hand" against his people? That's our problem, you see.
It seems that we've lost the accurate picture of the true
God of heaven and earth; we've substituted a god of
our own making. The true God deals in categories of
right and wrong, of truth and falsehood. God, in the
popular mind, is an enabler who helps us do whatever
our little hearts desire. That god does not exist; that
god is a pure fabrication. Maybe the reason people
have grown confused and complacent in the Christian
faith is that they have lost sight of the reality of sin
and judgment.

The sobering truth is that if God kept a record of our
sins, there would not be a person left alive among us.
"Cursed is everyone who does not continue to do everything written in the Book of the Law" (Galatians 3:10).
And we have not done them. That's the simple truth.

"You shall not misuse the name of the LORD your God"
(Exodus 20:7). Not only do we curse and swear falsely by
it, but we fail to call upon his name in every trouble, to
pray as we ought, or to give him proper thanks. "You shall
not steal" (Exodus 20:15), says the giver of all good
things. Yet we are not content with what we have. We

don't mind bending the rules if it means we will get ahead. Since it seems like everybody else is cheating, it becomes easier for us to cheat our neighbor as well. For each of us, there will be a day of reckoning.

Only Jesus has fulfilled the whole will and law of God. Dying our death in our place, he offered us his very own life to live. As a sign of his love and as an encouragement to our faith, he gives us a feast here in the wilderness of this world. What Moses, Aaron, Nadab, and Abihu could do only once, we can do over and over again. For as long as the earth endures, every time we eat the bread and drink the cup of the Lord in his remembrance, we eat and drink in the presence of God.

Thankfully, he does not lift his hand against us. There is pardon and peace in Jesus' name. There is comfort for every sorrowing heart and solace for every sinner crushed by the bitter memory of shattered promises. In that meal God himself gives us forgiveness of sins in the body Jesus gave upon his cross and the blood he shed for all. Along with forgiveness comes life—life to begin again. Life that loves what God has commanded and delights to do his will. A life that is not our own, but that comes alone through faith in Jesus Christ. We live his life with fullness, joy, and freedom in Jesus' name.

Lord God—the light of the minds that know you, the life of the souls that love you, and the strength of the wills that serve you—help us so to know you that we may truly love you, and so to love you that we may fully serve you, whom to serve is perfect freedom; through Jesus Christ our Lord. Amen.

St. Augustine

16. First the Cross, Then the Crown

Anyone who does not take his cross and follow me is not worthy of me. (Matthew 10:38)

The Scriptures teach, "We must go through many hardships to enter the kingdom of God" (Acts 14:22). And it's true. There is hardship, tribulation, and affliction in life. The personal burdens we bear and the tough times we endure are not accidental. Remember, Jesus said, "If anyone would come after me, he must deny himself and take up his cross daily and follow me" (Luke 9:23). First the cross, then the crown. We sometimes get it turned around. We'd like to go right for the crown and bypass the cross altogether. We prefer glory and honor over suffering or distress.

These crosses come in different sizes and shapes for each of us. For some it may be the cross of physical suffering; for others the pain may be emotional. It may be a constant struggle against bondage to sin or the prison of bitterness. For others the cross may be the chronic ache of loneliness or some other gaping hole in life that threatens to engulf us. But whatever the shape of the cross, still it is a cross, and it hurts. Suffering is not optional in the Christian life; it is one of the identifying marks of the Christian. To know Christ is to know the fellowship of his sufferings. The amazing thing is that these burdens are instruments of God's love and healing for us. We are not to shrink from our crosses nor retreat from our struggles.

God uses the hardships and reversals of life to crucify our sinful nature and drive us to his Word. God desires to kill the sin within us because it threatens our life with him. Through his Word our loving God brings us to repentance and encourages our faith. When we are broken and helpless, we often see God's love all the more clearly. Along with St. Paul, we learn that God's grace is sufficient for us. We see his power most clearly and seek it most earnestly when we are weakest. There's suffering of one sort or another in store for every Christian, but the sufferings of this present world aren't even worth comparing to the glories to be revealed in heaven's glory.

The path of suffering for the Christian leads ultimately to glory; that's the encouragement. But it is not our cross-bearing that earns us a crown, and therein lies comfort. For one day at Calvary all hell broke loose. All the ugly power of sin, death, and the devil was unleashed on God's own sinless Son. All the weight and burden of our guilt was heaped on him. God himself was given over into death so that he might give us his own life to live. First the cross, then the crown. And there is a crown for everyone who trusts in him; that's what lies ahead for all Christ's own. But not yet. None of us knows what life may bring. But we do know what Christ will bring. "Be faithful, even to the point of death," he says, "and I will give you the crown of life" (Revelation 2:10).

Gracious Lord, under the burden of bearing my cross, though the weight is great, I know I'm not lost. You designed my cross, so you know and understand my woe. You know how best to save me. I ask for your strength through Jesus my Savior. Amen.

Paul Gerhardt, adapted

17. Get the Picture?

Again he said, "What shall we say the kingdom of God is like, or what parable shall we use to describe it?" (Mark 4:30)

What is the kingdom of God like? To those on the outside looking in, the Christian faith appears to be a set of rules, a lifestyle, a system of right and wrong. Sadly, that picture leaves out faith, without which the whole of Christianity collapses like a deck of cards. Just what is this elusive thing Jesus called the kingdom of God? Our Lord was vitally concerned that you and I get the picture, so he gave us parables.

We don't do well with parables. We like lists a lot better. "Give me the facts, Jesus," we say. "Tell me what I have to do, and I'll do it. Teach me the five steps toward holy living. The six secrets of success. The seven principles for Christian witnessing." That's the way we'd prefer to have Jesus teach us about the Father and the work of the Spirit. We want easy lists or steps on how to fear and love God and to live under him in his kingdom. We prefer programs to truth.

Yet Jesus gives us parables so that he might teach us in picture stories what cannot be adequately described in ordinary language. "The kingdom of heaven is like treasure hidden in a field. When a man found it, he hid it again, and then in his joy went and sold all he had and bought that field" (Matthew 13:44). Get the picture? Jesus is that man, you see. He is the one who came searching out his own, to rescue and to save. He is the one, who for the joy that was set before him endured the cross, who emptied himself and lowered himself all the way to the death of the cross, that he might free us all from sin. Jesus our Lord paid for the whole world at great cost, freely laying down his life for us so that we might be his own.

Parables give us comfort and strength as God's people in our day. So rather than wringing our hands over the blatant immorality and godlessness rising all around us, it is time we find our strength and our peace in the Word of God and the sacraments. The gospel in Word and sacraments brings all the benefits of Christ's love— his forgiveness and his life to sustain us.

Finally, remember this parable: "The kingdom of heaven is like yeast that a woman took and mixed into a large amount of flour until it worked all through the dough" (Matthew 13:33). Christ will not abandon his church on earth. His church grows silently and oftentimes slowly. Yet it grows surely and steadily, sometimes in spite of us, producing a rich and bountiful harvest of souls purchased and redeemed by the innocent suffering and death of Jesus. We must have eyes of faith to see the glorious truths of what God has in store for his own. Our comfort is that what God speaks is sure, his Word is true, and his kingdom will grow and endure for ever and ever.

Father and God of all comfort, grant us through your Word and Holy Spirit a firm, happy, and thankful faith, through which we may overcome all trials; help us to realize that it is the truth when your dear Son, Jesus Christ, himself says, "Take heart! I have overcome the world" (John 16:33). Amen.

Martin Luther

18. Getting a Grip on Death

He went in and said to them, "Why all this commotion and wailing? The child is not dead but asleep." (Mark 5:39)

While the girl lived, there may have been hope, but certainly no longer. Her father's friends were critical: "Why bother the teacher any more?" (Mark 5:35). But Jesus ignored them. He heard them, and what they said made sense, but he ignored them. Instead, he turned to the grieving father and said, "Don't be afraid; just believe" (verse 36). Here we begin to get a grip on death. Getting a grip on death means to go beyond what we see. For God's things cannot be seen with the eyes; they must be received in faith. Jesus told the crowd that there was more here than met the eyes, "The child is not dead but asleep." They laughed at him.

Yes, they laughed at him, and people still laugh. Human wisdom always reacts that way to the message of the gospel. It seems absurd to the human intellect that God can take his Word, join it to water, and make it a bath of regeneration and renewing of the Holy Spirit. It seems downright crazy that the incarnate Son of God could give us his flesh to eat and his blood to drink under bread and wine. Human wisdom always leads us away from God. That's why Jesus said what he did to the grieving father, "Shut down your brain; turn off your emotions; stop fearing; just believe." In other words, "Trust me."

You can trust Jesus. He knows the threat and anguish of death. He's been there and back; he has conquered death. He commands us to stop fearing and then gives us the comfort of his promise at the same time. Not only does he command us to believe, but he also creates our faith. When Jesus speaks, things happen. In his mighty resurrection there is hope and promise for every heart still locked in fear and grief. Because of Jesus we have hope on the day we stand at the coffin of one we love or when we lay our head down upon our own death bed.

You can trust this Jesus of ours. You can trust him with your fears. You can trust him with your sins, and ultimately, you can trust him with your death. He handles all things on the basis of his own powerful Word. When you get a grip on him, you get a grip on death and, along with it, sin, shame, and fear. "I believe," we confess, "in the forgiveness of sins, the resurrection of the body, and the life everlasting." All these come from one living Lord and from his mighty, life-giving Word preached among us. Recall once more the powerful Word of the one whose living flesh still bears the scars of the death he died for you. Rejoice in his Word of life for you. Stop fearing. Only believe. And that Word shall raise you from the death of sin to newness of life, love, and hope.

Almighty God, source of all mercy and giver of all comfort, deal graciously, we pray, with those who mourn, that casting all their sorrow on you, they may know the consolation of your love through your Son, Jesus Christ our Lord. Amen.

Service Orders for Particular Occasions

19. God Works for Our Good in All Things

We know that in all things God works for the good of those who love him, who have been called according to his purpose. (Romans 8:28)

Is it really possible to say confidently, "What God ordains is always good"? Our hearts want to say "Yea and amen." It's just that the little word *always* sticks in our throats. Can it really be true that what God ordains is *always* good when often what comes our way hurts a lot?

Sooner or later a time comes in all of our lives when we're just plain up against it. A time when, despite our best foot forward and a good, stiff upper lip, we keep stumbling and sliding deeper into a gloomy pit of despair. What are we to do then? We would do well to look through the clear lens of the Word of God rather than relying on the distortions of human emotion. We can rarely trust our feelings, but we can always trust God's Word.

"In all things God works for the good of those who love him, who have been called according to his purpose." We might wonder if we love God enough so that all things will work for good in our lives. We need never wonder if we love him enough, for that kind of speculation leads only to uncertainty and despair. Rather, we find great relief and hope in the apostle's definition of those who love God as people "who have been called according to his purpose." We know for certain that we've been called. In Baptism, God calls us by his gospel and makes us his children.

At the baptismal font, he first called us by name. By the water, Word, and Spirit, he placed his name upon us, and we are born again. God the Father himself plunged us by Baptism into the death and resurrection of his own Son. Now dead to sin and alive to God, we have Christ's own life within us. We are being conformed to the image of God's own Son. We are becoming more like Christ, whose defining moment was his sacrifice and suffering at the cross of Calvary.

Suffering and the cross belong to us as well, because we bear the name of Christ. We begin to see his love most brightly when we have nothing but his cross to hold. In the hardships and reversals of life, we must look to someone other than ourselves for all that we need in this world and the next. In our hardships or afflictions, he is most pleased to claim us as his own and *in all things* work for our good. Always!

What God ordains is always good;
This truth remains unshaken.
Though sorrow, need, or death be mine,
I shall not be forsaken.
I fear no harm,
For with his arm
He will embrace and shield me;
So to my God I yield me. Amen.

Samuel Rodigast

20. God's Comfort

As a mother comforts her child, so will I comfort you; and you will be comforted over Jerusalem. (Isaiah 66:13)

I wonder how many men are man enough to speak about their love in such vivid terms that they would be willing to say they care for their children as a mother does? In this passage God does not shrink from using a female image to reveal to us something about himself.

"So will I comfort you," God says. And comfort us he does. The whole problem is that we don't like to admit we need any help. We're just not man enough— or woman enough—to admit that we need comforting. We are schooled to be self-reliant. We are brought up to handle things that come our way all by ourselves; we are expected to cope on our own. Oh, we get the message. No matter how devastating the blow, no matter how scary the situation, no matter how desperate the conditions, we try not to let on. We paste on our public smile and keep all our pain inside. "I can handle it," we keep saying. But we most certainly can't.

And we pay the price—not only in terms of ulcers, high blood pressure, and heart disease but also in terms of fear, anxiety, and distress. But these words of God come smack dab into the middle of all of our pain, fear, and loneliness: "As a mother comforts her child, so will I comfort you." It's just what we need, don't you see? The comfort of God.

The comfort God gives is more than a pious wish or a pat on the back. It's even more comfort than a mother's protective lap or her sheltering arms, where we were all held safe and secure, soothed and comforted in the midst of tears and terrors. God's comfort is found in a Man.

In one Man, Jesus Christ, all the fullness of God took up residence. Jesus didn't only talk about love, he loved the world in a most extraordinary way. "Greater love has no one than this, that he lay down his life for his friends" (John 15:13). Having said it, Jesus did it. Dying our death on Calvary's cross, he removed forever the penalty that stood against us. That's why you don't really know anything about comfort until you look at the cross of Jesus. At the cross you will find a comfort that is more than talk. God's comfort is genuine and can stand up in the face of the deepest sorrow and the sharpest pain.

God comes to meet and comfort us in his Word and sacraments. He dispenses his love, forgiveness, and life through the Word of his gospel, the washing of his Baptism, and the eating of his Holy Supper. Through these means we are given a share in the death and resurrection of Jesus, and we are comforted. In our God, who loves us, we find real comfort in the face of worry and sorrow. This is the God who comes to us with a comfort we can grab on to—a comfort much more real and lasting than comfort found in any mother's lap. It's the comfort we have in Christ Jesus our Lord.

Good Jesus, eternal Shepherd, I thank you that with your precious body and blood you graciously come to us in our poverty and exile and restore us. With your own lips you invite us to share in this mystery, saying, "Come to me, all you who are weary and burdened, and I will give you rest" (Matthew 11:28). Amen.

Thomas à Kempis

21. God's House of Prayer

And foreigners who bind themselves to the LORD to serve him, to love the name of the LORD, and to worship him, all who keep the Sabbath without desecrating it and who hold fast to my covenant—these I will bring to my holy mountain and give them joy in my house of prayer. Their burnt offerings and sacrifices will be accepted on my altar; for my house will be called a house of prayer for all nations. (Isaiah 56:6,7)

We seem to have forgotten what worship is all about. As someone put it, "We work at our play, we worship our work, and we play at our worship." It should not be so among us. We go to church because God is there; we go there to meet him and be transformed by him. The blessings come when worship becomes the highest priority. Those who serve the Lord, those who love the name of the Lord, those who worship him, yes, those who keep the Sabbath holy and hold fast his covenant—these, the Lord says, he will bring to his holy mountain and give them joy in his house of prayer.

But what is a holy mountain? In our human pride and arrogance, we've lost the sense of the holy. Our world doesn't know anymore what it means to be in the presence of God. This is perhaps the greatest tragedy of our secularized age. But the most serious loss and the greatest tragedy has been the loss of the sense of holy. We don't know where God is anymore. We don't have a place set apart and separate where we meet God. We've walled God out of our world. And if, by some chance, we have a place for God in our lives, we meet him not as an awesome holy God, but as a friendly buddy—only a little above us. There's little or no sense of accountability before God's judgment seat.

When God says, "You shall not," the sinful heart replies, "Well, I know a whole lot of people who do." When God says, "You shall not commit adultery," the sinful heart responds, "How can something be so wrong when it feels so right?" When God says, "Remember the Sabbath day by keeping it holy," the sinful heart responds, "But I'm busy that day." When God says, "You shall not murder," the sinful heart responds, "Unborn babies and feeble old people don't count." We could go on, but the point is clear. We've lost the sense of the holy, almighty, all-knowing God. The law of God becomes just another viewpoint, rather than the very Word of the Lord over all.

As Christians we have a different view. We go to church because it is a holy place where God is present. We find joy there, because there is joy in the presence of God. It's a deep abiding joy—joy that comes from having been in the presence of God. In his house we hear his Word and receive his sacraments. We, therefore, have the joy of sins forgiven and life restored. Joy that comes from forgiveness and eternal life is a foretaste of the glory of heaven itself. Church is a place holy with the gift of God's presence. His liturgy, worship, prayers, and praise are his gifts to his people in his Son, Jesus Christ, now and forever.

> O God, give me the joy of hearing your Word and help me to take root and grow in your church. Grant me grace to rejoice in its worship, and let not weariness and slowness of heart keep me from it. Open my mind to hear and to heed what you say to me today; through Jesus Christ my Lord. Amen.

Unknown

22. Good Intentions

Not everyone who says to me, "Lord, Lord," will enter the kingdom of heaven, but only he who does the will of my Father who is in heaven. (Matthew 7:21)

Generations of boys and girls who are now dads and moms or grandpas and grandmas stood once in white robes before the altar of God. They confessed their faith and pledged allegiance to the One who first washed their robes and made them white in his blood and clothed them with his perfect righteousness in the washing of Holy Baptism. For many of us, confirmation vows shaped our good intentions. Quite a mouthful of words are spoken at confirmation. We promised to use God's Word and the sacraments faithfully. We pledged to live our lives according to God's Word and remain faithful to God—Father, Son and Holy Spirit—suffering even death rather than fall away from him. We responded, "I do so intend by the grace of God." Remember?

That was our intention: to remain true to God the Holy Trinity and to the faith into which we were baptized. It was a good intention. The question is, what happened to that good intention? The sad truth is that over the years you and I haven't always continued in the pledge we made at our confirmation. We have despised preaching and the Word of God. We have often turned our backs on God's Word and sacraments, allowing other things to get in the way of being in God's house each week.

In fact, we have often mimicked the world instead of doing what we know to be good and right. We have set aside the things that are honorable and just in favor of what works. The things that are lovely and of good report are few and far between in our lives. We can barely hear the things that are excellent and worthy of praise any more; we've drowned them out with all the din and clamor of living in what we call "the real world." Our Lord would have us slow down and listen up.

Let no one despair. Let not your heart be empty or fearful or full of dread, wondering if your broken promises have ruled you out, wondering if perhaps you've wandered too far or stayed away too long.

Our Lord's promise to every tarnished sinner is that Jesus has shed his blood and enters into our hearts again this day by his precious Word and Holy Sacrament. In his redeeming love, we are pure, holy, and undefiled. The sins of the past have been bound to the cross of Jesus Christ our Lord. Satan is defeated and doomed to hell. The world will end in judgment. Yes, the power and peace of the forgiveness of sins in Jesus' name is our present comfort, our future hope, and our eternal joy.

> **Let me be yours forever,**
> **My faithful God and Lord;**
> **Let me forsake you never**
> **Nor wander from your Word.**
> **Lord, do not let me waver**
> **But give me steadfastness,**
> **And for such grace and favor**
> **Your holy name I'll bless. Amen.**

Nikolaus Selnecker

23. The Hammer of God

"Let the prophet who has a dream tell his dream, but let the one who has my word speak it faithfully. For what has straw to do with grain?" declares the LORD. "Is not my word like fire," declares the LORD, "and like a hammer that breaks a rock in pieces?" (Jeremiah 23:28,29)

What kind of God is this, whose Word consumes like fire and crushes like a hammer? The fact is that the same God whose Word is our comfort, our lamp, and our light is also the God of fire and destruction. He is both the God of fierce law and sweet gospel. Perhaps if we would just come to terms with the hammer of God, then the sweet light of God's holy gospel will become a more precious reality in our lives. If there is no hellfire, then the sweet calm of heaven means nothing. If God merely overlooks all sin and simply sweeps guilt under the rug, then the cross is robbed of all its power, and our faith is in vain.

We read in the letter to the Hebrews, "For the word of God is living and active. Sharper than any double-edged sword, it penetrates even to dividing soul and spirit, joints and marrow; it judges the thoughts and attitudes of the heart" (4:12). And we know what's within our sinful hearts, don't we? Greed and lust, envy and pride, idolatry and adultery—all this lies hidden deep in our hearts. The living Word of God is God's surgical tool to slice deep into the heart of our sin, attacking it with his clear word of judgment. No idle word, no casual selfish act, no deliberate or even unintentional rebellion against our holy God escapes his attention. "My Word," says God, is "like a hammer that breaks a rock in pieces."

God loves us too much to allow us to continue content and secure in our sin. And so God goes to work on us. He smashes our pride. God's law is harsh. It's summarized in the Ten Commandments. They are not the ten suggestions. They are commands God expects us to obey perfectly. Is it any wonder that God's Word is a hammer that breaks a rock in pieces? For the poison and filth of sin must be destroyed, and the hardness of human pride and arrogance must be demolished. Yet, through Jesus, God builds something new and holy and pure out of the wreckage of our lives and polluted hearts. So the hammer of God is his gift to us as surely as his forgiveness. The old Adam must be drowned daily so that the new man may emerge and arise.

At the cross all the power of sin to paralyze, all the power of death to terrorize, and all the power of hell to destroy is finished. At the cross God's love engulfed his wrath against our sin. God himself hung in agony on that cross to offer the ultimate sacrifice for our awful sin. He wrote "It is finished" indelibly with his holy, precious blood. So when the day comes that you live under the fire and hammer of God's judgment, remember that his Word is for you. Yes, God is serious about every sin we commit in thought, word, or action. But in his Word, God also tells us that Jesus has paid for every sin. In his Son, Jesus Christ, God says, "Fear not, for I have redeemed you; I have summoned you by name; you are mine" (Isaiah 43:1).

What God ordains is always good; his loving thought attends me. No poison can be in the cup that my physician sends me. My God is true; each morning new I trust his grace unending, my life to him commending. Amen.

Samuel Rodigast

24. The Harvest of Souls

The harvest is plentiful, but the workers are few. He who listens to you listens to me; he who rejects you rejects me; but he who rejects me rejects him who sent me. (Luke 10:2,16)

The Lord is not talking about oats or wheat. He's talking about human beings—the living souls who must be gathered into God's kingdom of grace before Christ returns to judge the living and the dead. There are plenty of people yet to be gathered. They are the living dead—alive in an earthly sense but dead in trespasses and sins. Living in ignorance and sin, they are lost in this world and have no hope for the next. The God of heaven and earth reveals his abiding wrath against those who get all wrapped up in themselves. They worship and serve created things rather than the Creator.

That's the way St. Paul describes the idolatry of his day, and that's the way it is among us as well. When we are distressed, we do not turn to him but to ourselves. When we are oppressed, we get angry and fearful. At such times we are unable to trust in the goodness of God.

All too often we find ourselves in this situation. God's gracious promises do not seem to be enough to carry us through. We become anxious and troubled about many things. We are afraid of what is ahead, and we refuse to be content with things as they are. Refusing to honor God, we find our refuge and purpose, our help and our hope in other people or things created by God. We don't find help in God, the Almighty Creator. Now if that isn't idolatry, I don't know what is. Put that together with all our other sins, and you have a pretty sorry mess.

These sins are too serious to be forgotten, too grievous to be ignored, and too dangerous to be overlooked.

That is why we too are part of the harvest. God sent his Son as the chief worker to gather in his harvest. He bore the heat and the burden of the day. He became a servant to us all. He humbled himself and became obedient unto death, enduring the cross, while scorning its shame. There, in that death of his, he died our death that we might live his life. Not only did the Father send the Son to gather in his harvest, but the Son also sent his disciples out to do the same—to gather in the sinners, redeemed and forgiven by the precious, holy, blood of Jesus Christ.

The power and authority of Jesus Christ to forgive sins has been given to the church, that is, people who believe in Jesus. The ministers God's people call continue to proclaim repentance and forgiveness of sins in Jesus' name. They speak not their own words, but Christ's word of forgiveness. And his words are spirit, and they are life. They are words of comfort and peace—words of hope and grace, life and light to those who abide in sin, darkness, and the shadow of death. In God's Holy Word and sacraments, there is life for all who live in death. It is the life of Jesus Christ.

Lord of harvest, grant anew,
Joy and strength to work for you,
Till the gath'ring nations all
See your light and heed your call. Amen.

Jonathan Bahnmaier

25. The Heart of the Matter

You have heard that it was said, "Do not commit adultery." But I tell you that anyone who looks at a woman lustfully has already committed adultery with her in his heart. (Matthew 5:27,28)

Jesus had a lot of gall. Can you imagine? The nerve of any man to stand up there and say something like that! "You have heard that it was said, 'Do not commit adultery.' But I tell you . . ." As if the commandments of the almighty God weren't enough. Now Jesus comes along and suggests that he can go one better. Indeed! Just who does he think he is, anyway? God?! Well, yes, as a matter of fact. This is the Word speaking here in the Sermon on the Mount. He is the Word, who was in the beginning and is God (John 1:1). And when the Word speaks, we listen. For when he speaks, he brings life.

But in order to do that, he first points out the living death in which we live. Those who heard Jesus didn't want to face that. Neither do we. We aren't much different from the people of Jesus' day. We'd like to think that we've got an inside track on the road to salvation because we've managed to keep our noses clean and our chins above the cesspool of sin in this world. We would like to think that our relationship with God is all a matter of our own doing. We are religious, moral, productive, and caring people. Surely that counts for something! Jesus informs us differently. He tells us solemnly that it's all a matter of the heart.

But . . . we protest. God's people aren't involved in sins of murder and adultery, are they? Jesus tackles the Sixth Commandment head-on in order to impress on us that our relationship with God is a matter of the heart. When he does, he makes it crystal clear that there is no one without sin on the strength of his own record. It's in our hearts that we have our problem with God. It is in our own urges and desires that all sins have their origin. Jesus points out that there's only one thing to be done with sin. It must be rooted out and destroyed. When we look into our hearts, we see that we cannot lead a holy and blameless life just by trying harder. The sooner we face up to the truth, the better. When we look toward our own hearts, we see that it's a hopeless case. No more hiding sin behind a fine religious veneer. When we look in our hearts, as Luther reminded us, we see only sin and death.

When we finally confess the truth about who we are—poor, miserable, damned sinners, murderers, and adulterers—Jesus has something else to say, "Blessed are those who hunger and thirst for righteousness, for they will be filled" (Matthew 5:6). "If we confess our sins, he is faithful and just and will forgive us our sins and purify us from all unrighteousness" (1 John 1:9). He purchased forgiveness for all our sins, and he means ALL sins—those we have tried to bury for so long, those that keep coming back to haunt us, and even those we've been afraid to admit. In his powerful forgiveness, he frees us. When Jesus frees us, we are free to live again—new, whole, clean, and pure. We live his life, which is the life of God.

> Almighty God, to you all hearts are open, all desires known, and from you no secrets are hidden. Cleanse the thoughts of our hearts by the inspiration of your Holy Spirit that we may perfectly love you and worthily praise your holy name, through your Son, Jesus Christ our Lord. Amen.
>
> *Late Gregorian*

26. Hunger for God

"For the bread of God is he who comes down from heaven and gives life to the world.""Sir," they said, "from now on give us this bread." Then Jesus declared, "I am the bread of life. He who comes to me will never go hungry, and he who believes in me will never be thirsty." (John 6:33-35)

The shelves of the mega-markets in our communities are overflowing with more food products than you could ever imagine. Our freezers are loaded with convenience foods. In seconds you can buy your choice of sandwich at a drive-through fast-food restaurant. So all this talk about hunger and food is pretty much like water off a duck's back. That is precisely why we, bulging with plenty and overindulged as we are, need to hear what God is telling us. Our loving God invites us to a fast, instead of a feast. He invites us to let go of all the delicious delectables of our consumer culture, to give up the attractive junk food of "stuff" on which we gorge ourselves in this idolatrous age, and to call a halt to all the conspicuous consumption. He wants us to be spiritual hungry again.

That's where we have to start, you see, with hunger. We need the genuine hunger of a spiritual fast. We need to break away from the idolatry to which we've become accustomed and to turn away from our fascination with created things so that we can focus our love and devotion on the Creator. That's what we need more than anything else in this world—hunger for God, a stomach-growling, voracious craving for God and the holy things of God. We need to be spiritually hungry.

The bread of God gives life to the world; it keeps a person going forever. So said Jesus to the crowd. But they had no spiritual hunger. They were only worried about their empty stomachs. We should be different. But the overindulgence, the conspicuous consumption, and the frenzied pace of our gluttonous age have dulled our appetite too. We are dying in this world. No matter how full of life we might appear, inside we are dying all the same. It's not just the loneliness and the heartbreak we face from time to time—even in the good times, when outwardly things are great. No, inwardly our sinful nature has no life at all.

What a gift, then, that Jesus personally invites us to live outside ourselves in him who died for us and rose again. All the life found in the fullness of him, he now extends and offers to us in his holy gospel. Jesus dispenses the life of God here in this dying world. Jesus himself invites you to leave your sin and live the life that he alone can give. He invites us to feed on his flesh and blood, given once for the forgiveness of our sins. Then we need to share the Bread of Life. Let those who are dying and starving in the wilderness of this world—those who are without hope and without God, those who hunger and thirst for righteousness— let them know what Christ has promised. "He who comes to me will never go hungry, and he who believes in me will never be thirsty."

We thank you, Lord, holy Father, almighty and eternal God, for satisfying the hunger and thirst of our souls with the spiritual food of your Son, Jesus Christ our Lord. Grant that our sins may be washed away, our faith strengthened, and our love for one another increased through Jesus Christ our risen Lord. Amen.

Unknown

27. The Implanted Word

Therefore put away all filthiness and rank growth of wickedness and receive with meekness the implanted word, which is able to save your souls. (James 1:21 RSV)

These words are as vital for us as they were to those first Christians nearly two thousand years ago. James, the brother of our Lord, provides apostolic direction, "Therefore, put away all filthiness and rank growth of wickedness." It's time to give up two-faced lifestyles, claiming to live as a child of God while flirting with the values and morals of this depraved age. It's time to stop playing fast and loose with the law of God.

Repentance, in other words, is where it all starts— good, old-fashioned sorrow over sin, a change of heart that leads to a changed life, a turning from sin to serve the living God. Repentance that turns from sinning to loving God with all our heart, soul, mind, and strength and then loving our neighbor as ourselves. That's repentance for you. It is literally for you, because through Baptism you are born again to a whole new life in Christ. That new life is by definition a life of repentance. It means the old Adam in us should, by daily contrition and repentance, be drowned and die with all sins and evil desires and that a new man should daily emerge. Because we live by faith in Jesus Christ in righteousness and purity, we rid ourselves of "filthiness and rank growth of wickedness."

But what then? What does the child of God do in the kind of world in which we live? How can we protect ourselves from the lies and temptations of our corrupt and depraved world? How do we go on living in this world and still avoid being contaminated by it? St. James directs us to the source of our strength, "Receive with meekness the implanted word which is able to save your souls." In that Word we rejoice, because that Word gives us the strength we need—Jesus Christ.

In Jesus Christ, the Father has opened his heart for all the world to see. Jesus Christ never changes. He died once for all, and his payment is as good today as it was centuries ago. The Holy Spirit has put Jesus in our hearts through the gospel. He is the implanted Word. The gospel is the power of God for salvation to all who believe—the power that works to turn us away from all filthiness and rank growth of wickedness. When we read, mark, and learn the Scriptures, the Holy Spirit continues to work and strengthen us so that we might live as Jesus desires now and eternally.

So we may either dabble around in the Christian life—as we tend to do when left to ourselves—or we may live the genuine life of repentance, receiving with humble hearts the implanted Word, which is able to save our souls.

Lord God, you are near to all who call on you in truth. You are yourself the Truth, and to know you is perfect knowledge. Instruct us with your divine wisdom and teach us your Word that we may know the truth and walk in it through Jesus Christ our Lord. Amen.

Christian Prayers after St. Augustine

28. In God's Household

Who then is the faithful and wise servant, whom the master has put in charge of the servants in his household to give them their food at the proper time? It will be good for that servant whose master finds him doing so when he returns. (Matthew 24:45,46)

There are many who worry that simple Word and sacrament have lost their effectiveness. They suggest that we must adopt an entirely different strategy as we prepare for the 21st century. In the text Jesus outlines a mission for his church that never changes. Christ's mission for his church was the same in the first century as it will be until he comes again in glory.

Jesus tells us what the church is: a household—God's household. It's not a social service agency or a political power base. The church is an oasis of God's life in a world of death. The church is an outpost of eternity in this world, a place of refuge from the storm. It is a place of comfort in sorrow, as well as a place of strength and healing in our human weakness and pain. In God's church the Holy Spirit, through the Word, provides the healing, the refuge, and the comfort of God himself. Notice what goes on in the church: the proclamation of the gospel, the washing of water with the Word in Holy Baptism, and in the Holy Supper, the eating of the body and blood once given and shed for us. These things are exactly what has gone on in the church for centuries. Some would tell us, "That's just the problem." Others say, "These things have lost their impact. We need something new and more interesting."

But what could be more interesting than to be in the presence of the Lord of all Creation? What could be more life-changing than to be baptized into the death and resurrection of Christ? What could be more revolutionary than to hear God's powerful Word proclaimed by his own servants? What could be more astounding than to have Christ's own body and blood placed in our mouths, the sign and seal of the forgiveness purchased upon his cross?

In God's household there is life. It is the life of Jesus Christ for the death of this world—for all those who struggle with the pain and suffering of this world, for all those who demand to have their own choice and make the wrong choice, and for all those who see their sin and repent of it. For each and every one of us who bears a load of deep and ugly guilt, there is life—righteousness in exchange for guilt, forgiveness in exchange for shame, and life in exchange for death.

That's what we need. And that's what the Lord of the church continues to extend here to us in the church, where the household menu is always the same. For there is only one food that satisfies and enables unto eternal life in this world of death: Jesus Christ and him crucified. Our Lord would have us come, eat, and live!

Remember, O Lord, your church. Deliver it from all evil, and perfect it in your love. Strengthen and preserve it by your Word and sacraments. Extend its borders so that your gospel may be preached to all nations. Gather the faithful from throughout the world into the kingdom you have prepared through Jesus Christ our Lord. Amen.

Swedish Liturgy

29. In Him We Are Worthy

People will be lovers of themselves, lovers of money, boastful, proud, abusive, disobedient to their parents, ungrateful, unholy, without love, unforgiving, slanderous, without self-control, brutal, not lovers of the good, treacherous, rash, conceited, lovers of pleasure rather than lovers of God. (2 Timothy 3:2-4)

Perhaps it is no surprise to you that polls show 79 percent of Americans agree there are no moral absolutes. What is alarming is that 55 percent of those in this country who call themselves evangelical Christians also believe that there are no moral absolutes. In our society nothing is unanimously condemned or rejected, except perhaps one thing. It is still forbidden to have a bad self-image. The cardinal sin in our world is to think of yourself as bad or unworthy. Everyone has an inalienable right to positive self-worth. The "self" has gone up on a pedestal in our age, and we are trained from little on to do homage to it. This is one great idolatry of our time.

God has words for such idolatry, and they are not pleasant words. They are words of judgment against our pride and arrogance. "Depart from me, you who are cursed, into the eternal fire prepared for the devil and his angels" (Matthew 25:41). We have a problem, you see. Despite all our vanity and arrogance, despite all our idolatry of the self and our cult of self-worth, the sad truth is that we are not worthy. We are not worthy to stand in the presence of God on our own because we worship a false god: the god of self.

There is One, however, who is worthy. And you know, of course who he is. "I am the First and the Last. I am the Living One," says Jesus. "I was dead, and behold I am alive for ever and ever! And I hold the keys of death and Hades" (Revelation 1:17,18). It is because he was slain that he is the worthy one. By his blood he has purchased us for God. From the right hand of the Father's throne, our Lord Jesus continues to dispense to his church the forgiveness of sins, life, and salvation, which he once earned upon his cross. And, wonder of wonders, the impossible happens. We, who are so tainted and polluted by sin and guilt that we cannot stand in the presence of God, are cleansed and made whole in Jesus Christ. Then he makes us to be a kingdom and priests to serve our God. In him, and in him alone, we are worthy—not in ourselves, but in him.

Already here on earth, it is the high privilege of the church's liturgy to echo the angelic song: "Worthy is the Lamb, who was slain, to receive power and wealth and wisdom and strength and honor and glory and praise!" (Revelation 5:12). Ours is only a dim echo of that eternal song that now rings in the presence of our heavenly King. But one day we shall see him as he is, and we will praise him as we ought, standing before his throne in heaven's glory.

To him who loves us and has freed us from our sins by his blood, and has made us to be a kingdom and priests to serve his God and Father—to him be glory and power for ever and ever! Amen.

Revelation 1:5,6

30. In Touch with Jesus

He went down with them and stood on a level place. . . . and the people all tried to touch him, because power was coming from him and healing them all. (Luke 6:17-19)

Have you ever noticed how important human touch can be? When we meet someone for the first time, we grip each other's hand; it establishes a bond of introduction between us. Researchers tell us that premature babies do much better when they are held and touched. Elderly residents of nursing homes seem to hunger for the touch of a human hand. It's no surprise that the people in the text were trying to touch Jesus. It wasn't enough for them to hear Jesus; they wanted to touch him.

Luke explains that power was coming from him and healing them all. I suppose that if you and I had been there, we would have wanted to touch Jesus too. But we weren't there. We are here. Yet we have the same needs as those in the crowd that day. Many of us are contending with sickness or disease. Some of us are struggling with loneliness and despair. Others do battle with the oppression of the devil, and every one of us contends with sin and temptation. We could use some power and healing. It would be nice if we could reach out and touch Jesus, but we can't. What's the alternative? Are we left to muddle along as best we can? Do we simply go to church week after week, hoping for the best? Thank God that the same Lord Jesus who reached out to touch the sick and hurting that day so long ago still reaches to touch us.

Time and space are no barrier to him. In his Word and holy sacraments, he breaks through the barricade of history to touch us with his healing love. He places his mighty Word within earshot so that by the power of his Spirit we may hear and believe. He puts his very body and blood, under the bread and wine, right in our mouths as pledge and promise of sins forgiven. In his Holy Word and sacraments, the King himself comes to meet with us. In the Word of forgiveness spoken by his called servants and in the proclamation of his gospel, Jesus himself acts to lift the burden of sin and guilt and to give life and freedom in exchange for death and bondage. Where there is forgiveness of sins, there is also life and salvation.

And if that's not power and healing, nothing is. You see, we are no different from the crowd gathered in the text. We come seeking healing, hope, and strength from the Lord Jesus Christ. Worn from struggle and fear, battered by sin and sorrow, we come with empty hands to receive his good gifts. Jesus does not disappoint; he makes good on his promises. Power comes from him to heal us all in the touch of his Holy Word and sacraments. Thanks be to God!

Almighty and eternal God, as you sent your only Son that we might see with our eyes, hear with our ears, and touch with our hands the Word of life, the eternal Christ, give us grace to receive in joyful faith the message of your Son, Jesus Christ our Lord. Amen.

Based on 1 John 1:1-4

31. Jesus Christ Prays for His Church

My prayer is not for them alone. I pray also for those who will believe in me through their message.
(John 17:20)

Jesus Christ prays for his church. If you've ever had someone tell you "I'll be praying for you," you know how comforting that is. But to have the Son of God praying for you is something else again. Maybe you didn't know it, but Jesus Christ prayed for you this morning. Jesus Christ prays for you this evening as well. In fact, he even prays through us in our prayers. That's almost impossible to imagine, isn't it?

The words of this text are really another prayer that Jesus Christ prayed for you long ago, the night before his death on the cross. Down through the centuries, the church has called this prayer the "High Priestly Prayer" of our Lord. Yes, Jesus Christ prayed for you that night, there in the upper room. Then he went out into the night for his betrayal, his arrest, his trial, and his death— his death for you, for the forgiveness of sins. But first he prayed for all those who would believe in him because of the message of the apostles. That night Jesus Christ prayed for his whole church throughout the ages.

And what did he pray? It would be nice to know that he prayed for your job security, your health problem, your happiness, or your prosperity. But he didn't. He prayed for the church's life. He prayed that the world might believe—the whole hurting, yearning, dying world. He has a peace and comfort to give that transcends the world's understanding. It's all found in him. All this peace and comfort, all the treasures of his love and forgiveness are found in the Lord of life who gave himself into death in order to free us all from the bondage of sin, death, and hell.

Jesus Christ prays for his church. He knows our sorrows and our weaknesses. He knows our hurts and our joys as well. But more than that, he works through the Word he has committed unto us, as well as through Baptism and the Holy Supper, which he has commended to us as his holy sacraments. Through these means our Lord enlivens us to do his will and enriches us with the forgiveness of our sins, with life and salvation. We are, after all, the very body of Christ, his hands and feet on earth to do his will. We are his church.

Jesus Christ prays for his church. Thank God, Jesus did not leave his church to fend for itself. Someone once said that God loved the world so much that he did not send a committee. Instead, he sent his Son, Jesus Christ, who prays that the world may believe. And that in believing we may not perish but have life everlasting.

Lord Jesus Christ, the Church's head,
You are her one foundation.
In you she trusts, before you bows,
And waits for your salvation.
Built on this rock secure,
Your Church shall endure
Though all the world decay
And all things pass away.
Oh, hear, oh, hear us, Jesus! Amen.

Johann Mentzer

32. Jesus Feeds His People

Taking the five loaves and the two fish and looking up to heaven, he gave thanks and broke the loaves. Then he gave them to the disciples, and the disciples gave them to the people. (Matthew 14:19)

What happened on the shores of the Sea of Galilee wasn't the first miraculous feeding, and it wouldn't be the last. The crowd had gathered in the middle of nowhere, a wilderness, and it was getting on toward evening. It was time to break up the meeting—the disciples informed Jesus—so that the people could go into town and buy some food. Jesus answered, "They do not need to go away. You give them something to eat" (Matthew 14:16). You know what happened. That day Jesus used five loaves and two fish to feed a whole multitude of people.

That's what happened then and there, but it has a lot of meaning for what goes on here and now. Jesus still feeds his people when we are in a desert place in our lives—at those times when we are all alone. We know there's a time and a place for being alone in the Christian life. In fact, when you're alone with God, it is good. But when you're alone by yourself, it's not so good. And many of us know all about that too. We tend to wall ourselves up with our hurt and our pain, feeling sorry for ourselves and nursing hatred and bitterness. That's not solitude at all; it's loneliness. Being alone without God is not good.

We need to be reminded that Jesus Christ is still with his people to feed and nourish them with his Word and the Sacrament, just as surely as he fed the crowd in the Galilean wilderness. Yet so often we forget that. Sometimes we think that Jesus is sitting off somewhere on the rim of a distant galaxy. We think that he has left us alone to struggle with our own fears and doubts. Then we are plagued by sin and temptations to sin with nothing but our own courage and our own inner resources to carry us through. We try to be more godly people, and we fall flat on our faces. Like St. Paul, we find that the good things we want to do, we don't do, and we wind up doing the evil things we don't want to do (Romans 7). Our inner resources are pretty flimsy when it comes to building a relationship with God.

That's why Jesus Christ feeds us in the desert places of our lives. He feeds us with his Word and the precious Sacrament. You might feel like you're deserted, but you're not. The Savior still comes to feed us in those private wildernesses of our lives. To every sinner weighed down by the guilt of the past or imprisoned in the bondage of present temptation, he says, "You're mine! You're free! Go and sin no more!" To every heart weighed down by shame or sorrow, stressed out by the anxieties of life, he says, "Come unto me, and I will give you rest." At times we all live in deserted places, all by ourselves. Remember, alone with sin is not good. But alone with God is very good. In those desert places within, Jesus Christ still feeds his people with his forgiveness, with his life, and his salvation.

Gracious Father, since your dear Son came down from heaven to be the true Bread, which gives life to the world: Give us this Bread, that he may live in us and we in him, Jesus Christ our Lord. Amen.

Australian Anglican Alternative Collects, adapted

33. *Lasting Fruit*

You did not choose me, but I chose you and appointed you to go and bear fruit—fruit that will last. (John 15:16)

The world we live in doesn't take kindly to people with convictions. No one minds if you profess the Christian faith; they just don't want you to be very serious about it. Sure, you can be a Christian, but the world would prefer that you don't live like one. Christianity, you see, is about truth, and the culture we live in isn't much interested in truth. It's more interested in feelings and personal opinions.

The whole concept of truth is up for grabs. That's why the truth of God and the commandments of God don't go over very well. That's why Christians are often regarded as quite peculiar because we believe that the living God, who made the heavens and the earth, has given us his Holy Word. That Word is objective, transcendent truth. Our lives of faith are built on the solid rock of the unchanging truth of God's Word in the face of sin.

That kind of faith can get you into trouble in this world. Most people aren't much interested in forgiveness and salvation. Instead, they're more interested in self-satisfaction and personal achievement. "Sin" is considered by many to be an empty relic of the past. No wonder, then, that forgiveness and salvation are scorned. For if there's no sin, who needs a Savior? But you and I know the truth. We know "if we claim to be without sin, we deceive ourselves and the truth is not in us" (1 John 1:8). More than that, if we say we have no sin, we make God himself out to be a liar. He has justly condemned the evil thoughts and actions that stem from our sinful hearts. Before his judgment seat, we stand convicted as rebels.

But God commends his love toward us in that while we were yet sinners, Christ died for us. He stormed the very gates of hell, crushed the head of Satan, vanquished death, and demolished the grave. Now he lives, nevermore to die. In him we too shall live. We are forgiven and restored. We become strong to live moral, Christian lives through the power only the Holy Spirit can give. This is the Christian faith.

But remember this: Such a faith is not of yourselves; it is a gift of God. "You did not choose me, but I chose you," says Jesus. He placed his name upon you when you were washed in the name of the Father, and of the Son, and of the Holy Spirit. Jesus has chosen you by his grace and begotten you again by water and the Spirit. Now he feeds you richly on his mighty Word and the holy, precious Sacrament of his body and blood. He will produce in you the fruits of faith in a life of service, love, and good works. He is the vine and will produce in you the fruits of faith. Those fruits shall remain. He who has begun this good work in you will bring it to completion in the day of our Lord Jesus Christ.

To him who is able to do immeasurably more than all we ask or imagine, according to his power that is at work within us, to him be glory in the church and in Christ Jesus throughout all generations, for ever and ever! Amen.

Ephesians 3:20,21

34. Let the Harvest Begin

I am the vine; you are the branches. If a man remain in me and I in him, he will bear much fruit; apart from me you can do nothing. (John 15:5)

Too often we fail. Our sinful nature gets the upper hand and we plunge into sin, doubt, and unbelief. Even though we want to bear much fruit for our Savior, we don't. Then we examine our lives and see that we can do nothing without Jesus. Our lives are filled with actions, words, and thoughts that reveal how helpless we are to overcome sin.

Where are the fruits of the kingdom in our lives? Where are the deeds of kindness, the works of love, the hearts and lives devoted to the Lord and his kingdom? Do our words and actions genuinely reflect our Christian faith, or are we simply living apart from Christ and living the same bleak life as others in this dark and godless world? Do we exhibit the godliness and holiness that belong to the citizens of a heavenly kingdom? Are our lives marked by chastity and sexual self-control, or do we simply live without regard for God? Is our language clean and above reproach, or do our mouths echo the obscenities and depravities of this godless time?

What about the people around us who are in desperate need for God? Do they find in us reflections of his love? Do the hurting find consolation in us? Do those in despair find hope and comfort in us? Do the lonely and the unloved find purpose and belonging? We are called to produce the fruits of the kingdom in our lives. We are called to put skin and bones on the love of God—to love our neighbors as we have been loved by God himself. We have the opportunity to comfort others with the comfort we ourselves have received from Christ Jesus our Lord.

Yes, we'll have to admit it: although we've been saying, "Lord, Lord," we have not been doing the will of the Father in heaven. We need to face the truth: Apart from Christ we can do nothing good. Admitting that before God is called contrition, or sorrow over sin. That's the first part of repentance. But the second part is faith, and that's the best part.

"If we confess our sins, he [God] is faithful and just and will forgive us our sins" (1 John 1:9). That's what he says, and that's what he does. Our Lord Jesus has purchased life for us all by his death. Not only did he make the perfect atonement for our guilt, but he also baptized us into his very death and resurrection so that he actually lives in us and we in him. When we fail it is all our fault because we still rely on our sinful weakness, but when we bear fruit, it is because Christ lives in us. The more we abide in him, the more fruit we bear.

Lord, take our minds and think through them. Take our lips and speak through them. Take our hearts and set them aflame with the desire to do your holy will; through Jesus Christ our Lord. Amen.

Unknown

35. By Faith or by Sight?

We live by faith, not by sight. (2 Corinthians 5:7)

How shall we live in this world that is passing away without being caught up in it? The answer lies in these words of God: "We live by faith; not by sight." Our skeptical mind replies, "More religious double-talk. What is all this talk about faith, anyway? What good is faith? It won't put food on the table or money in your IRA. Let's get real," we argue. "What's really important is what we touch and see and, above all, what we can feel. If we can *feel* something, then we can believe it."

The natural mind prefers sight over faith. There's just one problem. The natural mind is an enemy of God, the Bible says. That's why reason and feelings can never be trusted. Because in matters of salvation, they lead us astray every time. Reason tells us we're not so bad, especially when we compare ourselves to other people. Judging by sight, by outward appearances, sin is no real problem. Sure we sin, but so does everyone else. So what's the big deal about sin? That's the way our natural mind figures it.

Faith, however, believes the Word of God, and the Word of God says that sin is a big deal indeed. It is nothing less than idolatry and open rebellion against God. In fact, the wages of sin is death. That's how serious it is. Therefore rather than honoring our reason and our feelings, we honor the Word of God. Rather than saying, "I thank you, God, that I'm not as bad as other people are," we say, "God, be merciful to me, a sinner." We live by faith, not by sight.

Reason tells us that when it comes to the forgiveness of sins, Baptism is just plain water—a mere symbol of

69

personal commitment to Jesus. God's Word tells us that it is a "washing of rebirth and renewal by the Holy Spirit" (Titus 3:5).

Reason says that no one on earth can forgive sins before God in heaven. God's Word teaches us that Jesus has given his church the authority on earth to forgive sins (John 20:23). Jesus told his apostles, "He who listens to you listens to me" (Luke 10:16).

Reason tells us that the Lord's Supper is mere bread and wine. God's Word teaches us that the bread we break is a participation in the body of Christ, and the cup we drink is a participation in his holy blood, given and shed for the forgiveness of sins (1 Corinthians 10:16).

We live by faith, not by sight. Even when we can sense nothing in us but sin and death, God decrees it otherwise. If we confess our sins, God is faithful and just to forgive our sins (1 John 1:9). The forgiveness of our sin rests entirely on the work of God's Son, Jesus Christ. It does not rest on our thoughts or emotions. Because our salvation and forgiveness rest entirely on Jesus, it is absolutely certain. God has declared us to be holy, perfect, and righteous because of Jesus. Who will make God a liar?

I know my faith is founded on Jesus Christ, my God and Lord; and this my faith confessing, unmoved I stand upon his Word. Give me confidence in your promises, O Lord, that my faith may withstand every test and overcome every doubt. Amen.

Erdmann Neumeister, adapted

36. Living Happily Ever After

Then I heard every creature in heaven and on earth and under the earth and on the sea, and all that is in them, singing: "To him who sits on the throne and to the Lamb be praise and honor and glory and power, for ever and ever!" (Revelation 5:13)

The call goes out each night, as it will for as many nights as the church shall endure upon this earth to watch and pray. Guide us while waking, and guard us while sleeping. For those who watch, awake in Christ, may indeed rest upon their beds in peace. For Christ himself is our peace.

By the grace of God, we stand among those ransomed and redeemed. And so we commit ourselves, body and soul and all that is ours, into his powerful keeping, receiving from him the gift of quiet sleep. Each night we lie down in daily rehearsal of that day when we shall lie down in this world only to awaken in the next. So in our daily cycle—the ebb and flow of sleeping and rising again—we echo in our very bodies that grand and glorious day when Christ shall return again to planet earth. He shall come to awaken us and to judge the living and the dead. We await the glorious heavenly Zion of which the most splendid earthly mansion is but a distant and fading shadow.

And there, at last, God will keep us in the eternal perfection which he decreed before the world began. For this very reason he gave his only begotten Son—to redeem us all with his innocent death—so that we might live before him in righteousness and innocence forever. Yes, in other words, God decreed that we might live happily ever after.

Our home on earth offers only shadows of the things yet to come. In that world above, God himself will welcome home all who fall asleep in Christ. He himself will wipe away the tears from every eye, and death shall be no more. All mourning and crying and pain shall vanish. For the former things shall pass away. There we shall see what we now believe by faith. Now we see through a glass, darkly, but then face-to-face. Now we know in part, but there we shall know as we are known. When the kingdoms of this world become the kingdom of our Lord, it shall be farewell to these shadowlands below. But not yet.

All this awaits us, by God's own grace and promise, through his blessed Son. Yet now we remain steadfast in his peace. We find happiness already here and now in the anticipation of what is yet to come. St. Paul said it best, "For to me, to live is Christ and to die is gain" (Philippians 1:21).

We give thanks to you, heavenly Father, for giving us, in your great mercy, new life by raising Jesus Christ from death and filling us with a living hope. Let us finally possess the rich blessings that you keep for your people in heaven, where they cannot decay, spoil, or fade away. Keep us in faith by your power for the salvation that is ready to be revealed at the end of time. To you be the power and the glory forever. Amen.

Based on 1 Peter 1:3-5

37. The Man with the Right Answer

When Jesus saw that he [a teacher of the law, a scribe] had answered wisely, he said to him, "You are not far from the kingdom of God." And from then on no one dared ask him any more questions. (Mark 12:34)

They had been grilling Jesus on his knowledge of God. Can you imagine getting out your red pen to correct an exam taken by the Son of God himself? Jesus is the one who should have been handing out the grades, but the scribe proceeded to grade Jesus on his answer. The scribe, you see, thought Jesus might be the man with the right answer. But Jesus is not an answer man; he is the answer! There's a whale of a difference between the two.

Left to ourselves we all approach Jesus in much the same way as this scribe did; we ask a lot of questions, wanting Jesus to come up with the right answers too. Why is there so much suffering in the world? Why do I have to contend with the hassles I have in my life? How can I be the kind of person you want me to be? Just give me the answers I want so that I can improve myself. What must I do to inherit eternal life, Jesus? But Jesus answers such questions by reminding us we ask the wrong questions. A proper relationship with God is beyond our control. It's not something we do; it's something God does. It begins with love.

"Love the Lord your God with all your heart and with all your soul and with all your mind and with all your strength. . . . Love your neighbor as yourself" (Mark 12:30,31). That's all there is to a proper relationship with God. There simply isn't any more than loving God with all your heart, soul, mind, and strength, and loving others just like you love yourself. All the commandments can be summarized by absolute and total love of God and genuine love of the neighbor.

But we don't love, not as we ought. Not as Jesus outlines it for us. The arrogance of the human spirit puts its own will above the will of God and says, "My will be done, God, not yours." And that kind of arrogance and idolatry lies as much within our hearts as it does in the heart of every other sinner in our world today. The truth is, there isn't a person who loves God with *all* his heart and *all* his soul and *all* his mind and *all* his strength. The second truth is much like the first: there isn't a person who really loves his neighbor as much as he loves himself.

But Jesus Christ loved the Father perfectly, and he loved his neighbors as well, all the way to his death on the cross. He has taken our sin and death to his death so that we might live each day in the strength of his life. Our life is hidden with Christ in God. We live now in Christ by faith. Because Christ lives in us, we love God and our neighbors. Jesus is not the man with the answers for us to fix up our own lives. He IS our life. He's not the answer man, he is THE Answer. There is only one life to live in this world—the life we have in Jesus Christ—fed and nourished with his precious Word and his Holy Sacrament. The life we live is not our own; it's his.

Almighty God, as you yourself are love, fill us with the spirit of your holy love, so that our hearts may be warmed and we may forever love you and all people through Jesus Christ our Lord. Amen.

Cambridge Offices and Orisons, adapted

38. The Marriage Bed Undefiled

Marriage should be honored by all, and the marriage bed kept pure, for God will judge the adulterer and all the sexually immoral. (Hebrews 13:4)

Some people may find this text charming and dated—a little like a Victorian valentine, quaint but not too practical. Others may find it slightly embarrassing. But actually there's nothing either quaint or embarrassing about it. It's simply some straight talk from God about sex.

God's people can use some straight talk about sex. Today's Christians live in a world that is just as confused on the subject as the first century Christian world. In those days prostitution, extramarital sex, and homosexuality were rampant. Today, the situation has not changed, except that now we have an entertainment industry to glamorize it and publicize it.

The whirlwind of immorality and depravity we're witnessing is actually evidence of a society that is deeply empty and lonely. Desperately seeking closeness and intimacy, people look everywhere, but they find it nowhere. Wanting to be up close and personal, people try sex without commitment, and they end up even more alone and farther apart. The sexual aberrations of our age are wrong and sinful, but they're also extremely sad. In the dying world we live in, even this most intimate of human relationships has been twisted.

God will judge adulterers and the sexually immoral; it is true. Male or female, married or single, it's not easy to lead "a pure and decent life in words and actions." Yet God will judge us all, and his standards don't change. Yet that very fact is not only our warning, but our hope. For this Jesus Christ, who is the same yesterday and today and forever, remains faithful to us. We belong to him as members of his body (1 Corinthians 12:27).

This is the real reason Christians practice sexual abstinence before marriage and sexual faithfulness within marriage; we are already spoken for. The bodies in which we live are not our own. They belong to another, who purchased them at great price with his own blood once shed for us. These bodies are members of Christ himself; they are parts of his body. How can we use members of Christ's body for cheap thrills or selfish gratification?

The human will cannot corral the passions of the body and the lusts of the heart. Rather, chastity unfolds as we live out of the unseen realities of our baptismal identity. In Baptism we were consecrated as the pure and unblemished children of God. We grow into chastity as we grow up in every way into Christ. We receive in God's Holy Word and sacraments the power to crucify the old Adam; we put on Christ's gentleness, patience, and self-control. But whether married or not, we live as people who are already spoken for. Our entire spirit, soul—and body too—belongs to Jesus Christ.

> Eternal God, as you have taught us by your Holy Word that our bodies are temples of your Spirit, keep us temperate and holy in thought, word, and deed so that at the end we, with all the pure in heart, may see you and be made like you in your heavenly kingdom. Amen.

Brooke Foss Westcott

39. Mutiny in the Vineyard

Therefore I tell you that the kingdom of God will be taken away from you and given to a people who will produce its fruit. (Matthew 21:43)

Jesus told a parable about a vineyard that was beautiful and had rich, productive vines. But all was not well in that vineyard. The tenants plotted against the owner, rejected the servants sent to collect the crop, beat them up, and killed them. In desperation the owner sent his own son, saying, "'They will respect my son.' . . . But when the tenants saw the son, they said to each other, 'This is the heir. Come, let's kill him and take his inheritance'" (Matthew 21:37,38). And they took him and killed him. There was mutiny in the vineyard.

The story is transparent: the vineyard is God's people, Israel. When the Lord sent his prophets repeatedly over the centuries to preach repentance and faith, they were rejected. Some were beaten and scorned. Others were killed. Finally God sent his only Son. He came to his own people, but his own people did not receive him. Eventually they even killed him.

There is an unmistakable warning in our text. It is addressed to every smug, complacent sinner. When Jesus finished his parable, St. Matthew records that the chief priests and elders perceived that he was speaking about them. Yes, but he was speaking about us too. You and I cannot read this parable without asking about the state of God's kingdom among us.

The kingdom of God is, after all, here among us. Here God the Father continues to build his kingdom among those who will worship him in both spirit and truth. He bestows the forgiveness of sins through Jesus' blood to all who trust in him. Here the Holy Spirit calls, gathers, enlightens, and sanctifies his church on earth.

We must ask in our time whether we too have taken the Word of God and his kingdom for granted. What was true for the Old Testament tenants of God's vineyard is sometimes true for us. God will, in fact, remove his kingdom from those who do not produce the fruits of his kingdom. There is mutiny in the vineyard in our midst too. You and I are among the rebels who must come to repentance. We must turn away from our rebellion and sins and trust that God cleanses us from all unrighteousness. Then we will no longer live in our sins, but Christ will live in us. Jesus, our Lord, ever feeds and nourishes us with his sacred gospel in Word and sacrament so that we may be holy, filled to the brim with his very life and power. "If a man remains in me and I in him," says Jesus, "he will bear much fruit" (John 15:5). Such fruit the Father seeks and blesses.

As I pray, dear Jesus, hear me;
Let your words in me take root.
May your spirit e'er be near me
That I bear abundant fruit.
May I daily sing your praise,
From my heart glad anthems raise,
Till my highest praise is given
In the endless joy of heaven. Amen.

Anna Sophia of Hesse-Darmstadt

40. A New Heart and a New Life

Create in me a clean heart, O God; and renew a right spirit within me. (Psalm 51:10 KJV)

Those who are serious about repentance in today's moral climate will be swimming upstream. In the world we live in, it's not particularly fashionable to repent of anything. We're encouraged to assert ourselves, be good to ourselves, and to do whatever pleases us. But we are not deceived, you and I. Though we are in the world, we are not of the world. We have been born anew by the washing of water with the Word. We are children of the light, not children of the darkness. We know sin when we see it. It's just that we need God's courage to admit it.

When confronted with our sin, we usually go into the defensive mode. We have all kinds of excuses to offer. "Well, you know, God, I really meant to do the right thing. Even if I did the wrong thing." We console ourselves. "There were extenuating circumstances, you see, it was really my wife who made me do it (or my husband, or my boss, or that person I work with)." "It really wasn't my fault." Or worse yet, we go for a coverup operation. "It wasn't a sin. It was an error in judgment," we claim. "It was an unfortunate miscalculation." "It really wasn't so bad; lots of other people do things a whole lot worse."

Our God loves truth and hates sin. He threatens to punish all who transgress his commandments. And he means it. Our God heads right for the source of sin. Like a surgeon wielding a scalpel, our heavenly Father cuts deep with his Word to get to the source of sin, to get to the heart of the matter. Sin is deep inside us all.

We pray, "Create in me a clean heart, O God." We want to get to the heart of the matter too. We want to get at repentance, which means our cleansing and renewal in the name of Jesus. That is why Lent comes as such good news. We have the unique opportunity to come clean before God. It is a time to open up our hearts before our God and reveal to the bright light of his Word the sin and shame, the guilt and grief that are sealed up within. We need to get a new heart and find a new life. Repentance is just that, a time to turn from sin and to return to our God.

And God does not disappoint us. Though our sins are as scarlet, he makes them as white as snow, cleansed in the blood of Jesus his Son. God also gives us what we pray for and what we need so desperately—a new heart. For broken and contrite hearts find renewal in the Holy Spirit. By faith the Spirit gives us a new heart, righteous and holy in Jesus Christ. Thus the Holy Spirit renews a right spirit within us, which lives before God in righteousness and purity forever.

Almighty and eternal God, since you hate nothing that you have made, but forgive the sins of all, create in us new and contrite hearts that we may obtain from you perfect forgiveness through your Son, Jesus Christ our Lord. Amen.

Australian Anglican Alternative Collects, adapted

41. No Longer Living a Lie

Then David said to Nathan, "I have sinned against the LORD." Nathan replied, "The LORD has taken away your sin. You are not going to die." (2 Samuel 12:13)

As long as we say we have no sin, we lie and deceive ourselves. Our hearts remain proud and self-sufficient, and we continue merrily on down the path that leads to sure and certain death. But God intervenes. He comes with his law to break our hearts. He can do nothing with a hard and arrogant heart, but he can do everything with a broken heart.

King David is a perfect example. Now there's a man who lived a lie, if anyone ever did. After Uriah died, David's whole life became a charade. He pretended he was good and pious, but that was a lie. The truth was that he was a murderer and an adulterer.

Our sins may have different names, but we've all lied to ourselves and to God. The lies are familiar: "My sin isn't so bad; it's my wife's fault," or "I'm the way I am because I wasn't brought up right by my parents." There are other lies as well. We pretend that we have not really sinned. We begin to believe that we can solve our own problems, even as we sit in the middle of the wreckage of our lives, sorting through the rubble and trying desperately to put the pieces back together again.

But we're only fooling ourselves. The simple truth is that sin is sin and God is God. We know that God delights in the truth. That's why he cannot abide a proud heart. It is the same for us as it was for David. So God sent his prophet Nathan to confront David with his sin.

God crushes us under his judgment so that we are brought to nothing before him. "The sacrifices of God are a broken spirit; a broken and contrite heart, O God, you will not despise" (Psalm 51:17). Nathan was David's pastor. When David had come to repentance, he heard David's confession; then he pronounced the Lord's absolution. That's the way repentance works. First God had to crush David's heart; then he could make something new. So when God gives us a broken heart, we are on the path toward repentance and new life.

This new life is the life to live—no longer littered with broken promises and good intentions but the life God works in you through the gospel. This is no lie; this is the real thing. His love and his forgiveness rest securely in the suffering and death of Jesus. He poured out his life for you once upon his cross, but he comes here and now by his Word to fill you with his presence. By his grace and mercy, he declared you clean and holy in the truth of his forgiveness and gives you the promise of his peace. You have his very word on it!

Have mercy on me, O God, according to your unfailing love; according to your great compassion blot out my transgressions. Wash away all my iniquity and cleanse me from my sin. Create in me a pure heart, O God, and renew a steadfast spirit within me. Amen.

Psalm 51:1,2,10

42. The One Thing Needed

"Martha, Martha," the Lord answered, "you are worried and upset about many things, but only one thing is needed. Mary has chosen what is better, and it will not be taken away from her." (Luke 10:41,42)

I, for one, believe that Martha has gotten a bad reputation that she really doesn't deserve. She wasn't wrong in what she was doing. She just went at it with the wrong attitude. Jesus didn't condemn Martha for her work. Instead, he gently wanted to restore her priorities. We need our share of Marthas, after all, or no work would ever get done. We can't always be reading the Bible; someone has to take out the trash and change the baby. These works of love in daily life are part of our Christian vocation.

The faithful Christian is an arm of God's love as he or she serves others in doing faithfully the ordinary, routine things of daily life. Father, son, employer, employee, bank executive, dishwasher, CEO, or custodian—the vocation of every Christian is a holy calling. The reason is simple. Within the responsibilities of daily work and daily life, you and I serve as instruments of God to do his work. We provide for the needs and wants of our neighbors in the name of Jesus Christ! So let's set the record straight. It wasn't Martha's vocation that bothered Jesus, it was her attitude. "Martha, Martha, you are worried and upset about many things."

We understand. Much of the time we are worried and upset about so many things. We are often anxious and troubled about so much in our lives. We tend to excuse such worry, explaining away our fretting and fussing by calling it stress. But the dizzying whirl of our lives leads to more fretting, worry, and upset. And that is a sign. It is a sign that we have turned our lives topsy-turvy. We have lost sight of the most important things, and we have begun to focus on the wrong things. We have let go of faith in God and begun to trust in our own efforts and abilities. Let's call that kind of worry and upset what it really is—idolatry. It's what happens when we do not fear, love, and trust in God above all things, and when we begin, instead, to love and trust in ourselves above all things.

Jesus condemns our worry. Only one thing is needed. That's where Mary comes in. While all the bustle was going on around her, Mary sat quietly at Jesus' feet, listening to his Word. That was the one thing needed. It still is. For Jesus has reconciled us to the Father and declared us holy. Though there may be chaos all around us, there still is peace within. Peace established at the cross—signed, sealed, and delivered in the blood of Christ and conveyed to us here in his church by the gospel preached and the sacraments administered in his name. In that peace, joy, and strength, we lay our burdens down to listen when Jesus speaks.

One thing's needful; Lord, this treasure
Teach me highly to regard.
All else, though it first give pleasure,
Is a yoke that presses hard.
Beneath it the heart is still fretting and striving,
No true, lasting happiness ever deriving.
This one thing is needful; all others are vain—
I count all but loss that I Christ may obtain. Amen.

Johann H. Schröder

43. Open Ears and Loosened Tongues

People were overwhelmed with amazement. "He has done everything well," they said. "He even makes the deaf hear and the mute speak." (Mark 7:37)

The crowd that day was absolutely bowled over by Jesus. The poor man they brought to him for healing had never heard a sound since birth. Jesus took him aside and healed him. Pretty impressive, all right. The man was healed through remarkable means. First, Jesus put his fingers in the man's ears; then Jesus spit and touched the man's tongue. Finally, Jesus spoke a word: *Ephphatha*, which means "Be opened!" The crowd saw what Jesus did, but they didn't see who Jesus was. They saw the gestures, but didn't get the message: God has come down to planet earth in human flesh, and he has come to save.

Yet we can't be too hard on the crowd. After all, Mark records that the disciples of Jesus didn't get the message either. Jesus had to ask them about their own eyes and ears: "Do you still not see or understand? Are your hearts hardened? Do you have eyes but fail to see, and ears but fail to hear?" (Mark 8:17,18). So often we too live as though it's all up to us to handle the hassles and burdens of life all on our own. "I am with you always," Jesus assures us, but our ears are deaf to his promise. So often we live as though we have been abandoned, salving our pain and loneliness with self-pity. "Take heart," Jesus comforts us. "Your sins are forgiven." But so often we lug around the burden of guilt we've accumulated over the years, our own private, ugly collection of sin, which the devil uses to undermine our hope and drive us to despair.

"Be opened!" Jesus says to us today as well. For we have ears that so often fail to hear the message he addresses to us. We have eyes that so often fail to see the power of Jesus revealed in his Word and sacraments. Jesus still uses remarkable means for healing. The water of Holy Baptism and the bread and wine of the Holy Supper are the very vehicles of Christ's full and complete forgiveness. Together with the preaching of the gospel, these sacraments extend the power of Jesus right into our lives. Jesus uses his Word and sacraments to apply all that he has earned for us in another place and time to us right here and now.

Jesus speaks his word to us, "*Ephphatha! Be opened!*" He endured the cross and grave so that he could speak that word. And he gives us ears to hear his Holy Word and hearts to believe his promises. He gives us tongues to speak in witness and in praise.

By the power of the Holy Spirit through the gospel, suddenly ears can hear again. He loosens our tongues and opens our mouths to sing his praise and tell of the wonderful deeds of our Savior, who brought us out of darkness and silence into his marvelous light.

God be in my head and in my understanding;
God be in my eyes and in my looking;
God be in my mouth and in my speaking;
God be in my heart and in my thinking;
God be at my end and at my departing. Amen.

Sarum Primer, 1558

44. Open-Mouthed Praise

O Lord, open my lips, and my mouth will declare your praise. (Psalm 51:15)

There is an old saying in the church that all theology is doxology, that is, all words about God are words of praise. Thus it is only fitting that we begin each day with words of praise about God that come from God. Even in our worship, the words of praise we say and sing are not our own. They are words from God.

Left on our own, we have no praise to bring. The sinful heart dare not speak of God, except in fear and dread. Our proud knees cannot bend to pray. Our haughty hearts do not stoop to worship. Our sin-polluted mouths rebel and refuse to speak God's praise. Therefore the psalmist teaches us how to pray. He begins at the beginning. He begins not with man, but with God. "O Lord, open my lips." First things first, you see. If we look at Psalm 51, the very first thing we see is the confession of sins, which is the beginning of praise. "Have mercy on me, O God, according to your unfailing love; according to your great compassion blot out my transgressions. Wash away all my iniquity and cleanse me from my sin. For I know my transgressions, and my sin is always before me" (verses 1-3).

That's not the way we would like to begin our praise. The human heart, in its pride, prefers to jump over such unpleasantries and go for the good stuff. We'd like to think that we're doing God a favor in our worship. He should be flattered by our praise, as if he's just sitting around in heaven, idly waiting for the show to begin. Then when it's over, we expect him to applaud politely at the effort we've put into our worship. Such is the height of human arrogance, the depth of human sin.

Man-centered worship is flimsy stuff indeed. It's no wonder that the psalmist leads us to solid ground. He leads us to the forgiveness of sin: "Cleanse me with hyssop, and I will be clean; wash me, and I will be whiter than snow. Hide your face from my sins and blot out all my iniquity. Create in me a pure heart, O God, and renew a steadfast spirit within me" (Psalm 51:7,9,10). God shatters our private prison cell of shame and remorse, opening his gates of praise to the likes of us. God has freed us from our sins and ransomed us with the blood of Christ. He has buried us by Baptism into his death and wrapped us in his risen life. By that gospel he has pried open our stony hearts and given them faith and a song to sing. He has opened our lips that we might praise him now and forever.

Oh, keep us in your Word, we pray;
The guile and rage of Satan stay!
Oh, may your mercy never cease!
Give concord, patience, courage, peace. Amen.

Nikolaus Selnecker

45. Antidote to Death

Just as Moses lifted up the snake in the desert, so the Son of Man must be lifted up, that everyone who believes in him may have eternal life. (John 3:14,15)

The people of Israel, bitten by poisonous snakes, were dying like flies. They appeared to be doomed. The horrible thing was that Israel deserved to die because they despised God's grace. They had forgotten their slavery in Egypt, and they had forsaken the God who rescued them and miraculously delivered them. Such open defiance, such arrogant, impenitent sin could not be ignored. You cannot renounce the life God gives and go on living. God's eternal decree is "The soul who sins is the one who will die" (Ezekiel 18:4).

The snakes were no mistake; the Lord himself had sent them. Yet as God gave death to the impenitent, he also gave life to those in sorrow over their sin. He provided the remedy for sin—a bronze serpent—the antidote of life. If a snake bit someone, he could look upon the bronze snake and live. The snake on a pole was a preview of what would happen on Calvary's cross.

As it was for Israel, so it is for us. God rescued us from bondage to our sin by the waters of Holy Baptism, where all our sins were drowned. In Baptism we died once with Christ and were raised again to live as new creations in him. From the altar, we are given to eat the very body and blood of our Lord Jesus Christ himself. He feeds us here on earth with the holy food that endures unto life eternal. But we, like Israel, grumble and complain; we gripe and moan. When hardship comes our way, we're the first to ask, "Why me?" We doubt the promises of God; we turn our backs on his

Word, and we turn up our noses at his sacraments. Though he repeatedly promises, "I will never leave you," we insolently ask, "God, where are you?"

We too have transgressed God's commandments. And the penalty is still death. But there is an antidote to the death you and I deserve. "God demonstrates his own love for us in this: While we were still sinners, Christ died for us" (Romans 5:8). His death is the means to life for us all. As Moses lifted up the snake in the desert, so Jesus was lifted up upon his cross to be death's antidote for us all. God's promise continues, "that everyone who believes in him may have eternal life."

Let no one doubt the love of God. Let no heart, torn and distressed by life, be lost in despair and fear, thinking there is no hope. Do not think you're all alone and desolate in the wilderness of this world. Let no one, broken and crushed under the pressure of living, be crushed under the bitter weight of sin and shame. For Jesus, the very Lamb of God, was lifted up upon his cross to bring you life and light this very day and for all eternity.

Merciful Father, give us grace that we may never deliberately sin. But, Lord, if at any time we offend your majesty, may we truly repent, lament our offense, and by a living faith, obtain forgiveness of all our sins, solely through the merits of your Son, our Savior Jesus Christ. Amen.

Book of Common Prayer, 1549

46. The Perils of Possessions

As Jesus started on his way, a man ran up to him and fell on his knees before him. "Good teacher," he asked, "what must I do to inherit eternal life?" ". . . Children, how hard it is to enter the kingdom of God! It is easier for a camel to go through the eye of a needle than for a rich man to enter the kingdom of God." The disciples were even more amazed, and said to each other, "Who then can be saved?" Jesus looked at them and said, "With man this is impossible, but not with God; all things are possible with God." (Mark 10:17,21-27)

Our Lord Jesus preaches the law as well as the gospel in this text, and some of us would rather not hear the law. Some of us have the idea that the church's job is to give people a nice, comfortable religious feeling that God's in his heaven and all's right with the world. Well, all is not right with the world. If the world did not need redeeming, God would not have sent his Son here in the first place. If all's right with the world, there would be no judgment day to come, and there would be no Savior. If all were right with the world, God would not have resorted to such a drastic method of saving the world; there would be no need for the cross. If sin were no big deal, God himself would not have had to die in order to save us all.

Take the man in the text, for example. All was not right with him either. He was an intense, eager, likeable guy who had worked hard at truth, integrity, godliness, and honor. The man was absolutely sincere and wanted to know what to do to inherit eternal life. Like some of us, he favored a plan for salvation in which God helps those who help themselves. There was just one problem; he had the wrong God. "One thing you lack," Jesus said. "Go, sell everything you have and give to the poor, and you will have treasure in heaven. Then come, follow me." The man went away sorrowful, St. Mark records, because he had great possessions.

There is a peril to possessions as far as the kingdom of God is concerned. Possessions have a way of replacing God. If we stop for a moment and consider how much time and energy we put into accumulating and maintaining our earthly possessions and how much time we spend building and strengthening our relationship with God through his Holy Word and the Sacrament, the contrast becomes fairly obvious. We so easily fall into idolatry when it comes to our possessions. The peril is that in gaining the world, we might lose our own soul. Which is more important, after all—the things we accumulate or our gracious God and his Holy Word?

Let the idols of possessions, the wealth of this world, come crashing down. Let us use all the good gifts God gives us in this world. But we must remember, they are tools to use for his glory, not ends in themselves. Let God be God. Let us give our worship, adoration, and devotion to him alone. All things are possible with God. God makes sinners righteous, and he raises the dead to life in Jesus Christ. Now being raised to life, let us live in him, for him, through him—and him alone!

Gracious Father, as you have so generously placed in our hands the wealth we call our own, help us to manage our possessions wisely so that they may not be a curse in our lives, but an instrument for blessing through Jesus Christ our Lord. Amen.

Australian Anglican Alternative Collects, adapted

47. Poor, Captive, and Needing Rescue

The LORD has anointed me to preach good news to the poor. He has sent me to bind up the brokenhearted, to proclaim freedom for the captives and release from darkness for the prisoners, to proclaim the year of the LORD's favor. (Isaiah 61:1,2)

One day Jesus worshiped at a synagogue in Nazareth. The scroll of the prophet Isaiah was handed to him, and he read the words recorded above. Then he did the unexpected. He said, "Today this scripture is fulfilled in your hearing" (Luke 4:21).

"How could he?" they must have thought. What gall! Who does he think he is?

We've gotten over the shock, but we still have a question. "Who are these tragic and needy people?" we ask. The down and out? The addicted maybe? The scum of the earth or the dregs of society perhaps, but surely not us.

In all of God's Word, we need to hear both the good news and the bad news. The bad news is this: YOU are the one of whom Jesus speaks. You are both poor and captive. Yet the good news is that God has come for such as you.

The truth is that we are all poor, indeed, when it comes to God. We have wandered, every one of us, to his own way. We are captives as well to the wild impulses of our sinful nature. Despite our best intentions, we often relish the very thoughts and actions of which we ought to be ashamed. We find a way to yield to the temptations of the devil. We allow the dictates of a sinful heart to take over, and we cave in to the lusts of our sinful nature. Yet we enjoy it so. At times we even pretend that we are good and holy, when in fact there is nothing good that dwells within us, that is, in our sinful nature. We are captive to our sin, even if we deny it.

We need to confess our sin and to hear Christ's word of absolution. The Spirit breathes life into the likes of us, lost in sin and death as we are. We have nothing to bring him, except our empty hands and our shattered hearts. But in such he delights. For the sacrifices of God are a broken spirit and a contrite heart. When we are nothing, then he is everything. In the very midst of our nothingness, he is our everything. As long as we remain smug, complacent, and proud in our sin—as long as we remain full of ourselves—we cannot be full of him. But when we are empty and come to him, crushed and desolate with contrite hearts, then he is faithful and fills us to overflowing with his forgiving love.

For this Christ came into the world so long ago. The Lord Jesus was born in a stable and nailed upon a cross so that he might be the life of all of the living and the death of death. He absorbs into his holy body all the sin and death that dwells within us and abolishes the whole rotten mess of our captivity to sin by his cross and death. His great gift to us is his healing, his freedom, and the richness of his grace.

> Love caused your incarnation;
> Love brought you down to me.
> Your thirst for my salvation
> Procured my liberty.
> Oh, love beyond all telling
> That led you to embrace
> In love, all love excelling,
> Our lost and fallen race! Amen.

Paul Gerhardt

48. The Pursuit of Happiness

A man's life does not consist in the abundance of his possessions. (Luke 12:15)

You won't find these words in the *Wall Street Journal* nor in the pages of any magazine for upwardly mobile people. These words are the Word of God, and when God speaks we take notice. The issue our Lord would have us examine is how we are to live in a land where we have so much. Now our first reaction is to dispute that. "I can think of all kinds of things I don't have," we object. That's just the point. We always want more. An endless struggle for more is just as spiritually dangerous as having too much. The temptation in our world is simply plain old-fashioned greed—putting created things on a higher pedestal than the Creator himself. Greed is, after all, idolatry.

We must confess that our culture breeds idolatry. It's not that we carve idols and hide them away in our closets to use in strange rituals. The idolatry of greed is much more subtle, but just as sinister. It would have us believe that we are nobodies without the right homes or the right clothes. Bit by bit we become convinced that genuine happiness can be found in things, rather than in the God who gave these things to us. It's time to call that what it is—a damnable lie. Clearly it is not the truth of God, and the lie comes straight from the devil.

How are we to live in a world where we have so much? We must begin with repentance. We begin by taking honest stock of where we have been and where we are with this demonic lie that life consists in the abundance of possessions. For all idolatry is sin, and there's only one thing to be done with sin. Confess it. If we confess our sins, God is faithful to forgive our sins and cleanse us from all unrighteousness. He who is God in flesh forgives sins, because he bore them in his flesh and died our death, giving us his new life to live.

Therefore we can say no to sin and the seduction of greed. We say no to the lie that life consists in the abundance of possessions. We refuse to buy the lie that happiness can be bought and sold.

Do you want to know the secret to true happiness and fulfillment? Quit looking for something out there somewhere that will give you genuine happiness; look to what you already have in Jesus Christ. We have our whole identity and fulfillment in him. By Baptism he has wrapped us up within his death and made us his own. Then, freed from the struggle to acquire, we are truly free. Free to live contented lives, we, therefore, faithfully keep on doing what we have been given to do in daily life, knowing that all good things come only from the hand of God. This is where true happiness is found.

Lord, my God, rescue me from myself and take away from me everything that draws me from you. Give me all those things that lead me to you; for Jesus Christ's sake. Amen.

The Latin Precationes Piae, 1564

49. Remember to Remember

When you have eaten and are satisfied, praise the LORD your God for the good land he has given you. Be careful that you do not forget the LORD your God, failing to observe his commands, his laws and his decrees that I am giving you this day. (Deuteronomy 8:10,11)

We live among people who have failed to remember. We live among people who have forgotten the Lord our God. We live in a time when the commandments, laws, and decrees of God have been set aside. This is a time when everyone seems to do what is right in his own eyes. Even people of faith have begun to compromise the Word of God and, instead, to live by the inclinations of their own sinful hearts. Each person has become his own authority—what he or she feels or thinks is held to be right, whether or not it corresponds to the will of God. We are guilty of exalting our own personal preferences and our own personal emotions over the Word of God. Remember, the Word of God is the final judge of human opinion, not the other way around.

Remember not only the Word of God but also the gifts of God. Scripture is clear that to whom much is given, much is required. Too easily do we begin to take our Lord's gracious gifts for granted. Too easily we assume that we deserve all our belongings because of our hard work and dedication. Then pride takes over for faith as we begin to believe that the credit is ours rather than God's. The next step follows quickly. We turn our backs on the God who gives all. It is he, not we, who must be exalted as we remember the gifts of God. Jesus is the greatest gift of God. From him and his work all other blessings flow. Laying down his life for us all, he gave himself over to die our death. In so doing he has given us life never-ending.

Remember the many gifts of God that flow from Jesus. In the gospel—the message of God's love for us sinners—God himself speaks to our hearts to forgive our sins. When called servants proclaim that gospel, God speaks and works. In the washing in the name of Father, Son, and Holy Spirit, the Holy Trinity adopts sons and daughters as his own and gives them to share in his unending life. In, with, and under the bread we eat and the wine we drink, we have the very body and blood of Christ, given once for all for the forgiveness of sins. These are the wonderful gifts of God that we all too often take for granted and forget.

As we look into the 21st century, we open the door to the future. Whatever may come our way, we face it all fearlessly in the strength of him who has given us all. We will remember. We will remember to remember the Word of God and the gifts of God. By that Word and his gifts alone we live.

Lord Jesus Christ, as you have said that you are the way, the truth, and the life, let us never stray from you, the way, never doubt the promises given by you, the truth, nor rely on anything else than you, the life; for without you there is nothing to be desired in heaven or on earth. In your name we pray. Amen.

Christian Prayers, 1578

50. Repent

From that time on Jesus began to preach, "Repent, for the kingdom of heaven is near." (Matthew 4:17)

"Repent." That's how Jesus began his preaching, and that's how he continued to preach. Do you think Jesus would be a popular preacher today? I'm not so sure. We like to be told how good we are, not how bad we are. We like to be told what we can do to improve our own situation; we don't like to be told that we can do nothing. We like upbeat sermons; yet Jesus began in a rather downbeat way. "Repent," he said.

Could it be that Jesus was wrong? Of course not. It's you and I who are wrong. It's whole segments of our world and Christendom that have gone wrong. Looking for a quick fix for our predicament, we have swallowed lies. Some believe that we can improve our own lot by moral reform. Others believe that happiness and fulfillment are do-it-yourself projects. Still others believe that we can clean up our own lives and straighten out our own mess if we just have the right information and the desire to carry it out.

But these are all lies. Lies straight from hell and the father of lies, the devil. For the Bible says exactly the opposite. "You were dead in your transgressions and sins" (Ephesians 2:1). Dead! As in without life, movement, will, or desire! Even when God works the miracle of faith in our hearts, we often have the desire to do what is right, but we cannot carry it out. That's what the apostle Paul tells us, speaking by inspiration of the Holy Spirit (Romans 7:18). And that's the truth.

God loves the truth. That's why he always begins with the law and ends with the gospel. First the truth about who we are and what we have done, then the truth about who he is and what he has done. First his judgment, then his grace. First the demolition, then the reconstruction. First his wrath against our sin, then his love by which he creates us all over again in righteousness and true holiness in his holy Son, Jesus Christ.

Jesus means precisely what he says, "Repent." He intended that our whole life be a life of repentance. It's a daily, continuous return to our baptism, where our old Adam was first put to death, buried along with Jesus into his death, and a new self was raised up again along with Jesus to live his new life. As long as we live in this world, day by day, the old sinful self in us needs to be put to death anew. How? By contrition and repentance.

Repentance is nothing less than God's work of grace through which he gives us a whole new mind, heart, and life. The life we live in Jesus Christ our Lord, God works in us by his precious Word and holy sacraments; that life is ours to live anew today!

Heavenly Father, we thank you for our baptism, in which you have forgiven our sin, delivered us from death and the devil, and given us everlasting salvation. Grant that our sinful self, with all its evil deeds and desires, be drowned through daily repentance; and that day after day a new self should arise to live with God in righteousness and purity forever. Amen.

Based on the Blessings and Meaning of Baptism from Luther's Small Catechism

51. Rest for the Weary

Come to me, all you who are weary and burdened, and I will give you rest. (Matthew 11:28)

When Jesus says, "weary and burdened," we're all ears. That's us. We are weary and burdened. It's not just the burden of our daily work. No, it's the weariness of living. We sometimes get downright sick and tired of everything. We scramble so fast in this world of ours, just going about the business of living, that the whole concept of rest seems foreign to us.

What can be done about it? Many people believe that the Christian faith is supposed to do the trick. Faith in Jesus will help us find a silver lining for every cloud. The trouble is that life doesn't work that way. Sheer willpower will not turn our frowns upside down into happy smiles for Jesus. The Christian church is not a big self-help group, where we simply forget our troubles by thinking happy thoughts to chase the blues away. Fortunately, Jesus has something better for us than simply happy thoughts. He gives us himself.

"Come to me," he says, "and I will give you rest." It's important to hear him clearly. Left to ourselves we really don't want rest from Jesus; we want rules. We'd like to know what we can do to improve our situation, what we can do to become healthy, wealthy, and wise. We would like Jesus to give us a 12-step recovery program. At minimum, we want to know what we can do to clean up our act and make ourselves over into better people. But Jesus is not a moralist. He is a Savior!

It sounds strange to hear Jesus first invite us to rest and then in the next breath to say, "My yoke is easy and my burden is light." How can a yoke be easy or a burden light? When it is the yoke and burden of Jesus; that's when! It is the yoke of the cross. On his cross Jesus pulled off the greatest swap in history. He took our sin and gave us his own righteousness. He took all our sin away with him into his death. His cross, that sign of death, is the sign of life and healing for us. This is what it means to be a Christian, to be baptized into the death and resurrection of Jesus, to bear the mark of the cross in this world. This is our calling. This is our yoke, but it is also our deep and abiding joy. For every burden there is strength, in every sorrow there is comfort, and in all distress there is peace. It is the strength, comfort, and peace of Jesus Christ.

Wherever Jesus is, there is rest for weary hearts and burdened souls. He is present among us, offering a Sabbath rest for all the people of God in this world. We have the high honor to come to Jesus where he has promised to be found—in his holy church, where his Word is preached and his sacraments administered. There he continues to bring healing for weary hearts and strength for burdened souls.

Blessed Lord, grant that in the midst of our work, we may find rest and peace in your presence and may take joy in serving you, our refuge, our strength, and our great reward. Amen.

Unknown

52. The Sabbath Lord

The Pharisees said to him, "Look, why are they doing what is unlawful on the Sabbath?" Then he said to them, "The Sabbath was made for man, not man for the Sabbath. So the Son of Man is Lord even of the Sabbath." (Mark 2:24,27,28)

We have a way of taking some of the best blessings of God and turning them into burdens. Children become obligations. Before we know it, friends become competitors, and work becomes a chore. Take the Sabbath, for example. God gave the Sabbath to his people as a gift, not an obligation. "Remember the Sabbath day, by keeping it holy," God said in the Third Commandment. Yet the Lord's day becomes an intrusion; it cramps our lifestyle. "Me, go to church? Worship? I need my weekends to rest."

God really intended the Sabbath to be a blessing for his people. It was, indeed, a holy day—set aside and apart for God. Remember that on the Sabbath the great, powerful God himself paused from his work of creation. So God gave the Sabbath rest to his people as well. Once every seven days, they were to pause from their normal labor, to rest weary bodies, and to refresh weary souls in his presence. It was literally a day marked uniquely by the Word of God and worship.

But sure enough, God's people made his gift into an obligation, adding all kinds of rules and regulations. The rules God's people created even specified, for example, how far one could walk on the Sabbath day and technically still keep the law. They wanted to earn God's approval by keeping every regulation. And so Jesus was criticized in the text because his disciples were plucking the heads of grain along the road on the Sabbath and munching on them. In the Pharisees' eyes, he was undermining the Sabbath and breaking the rules. The Sabbath was an obligation to them.

But we're not that much different. God gives us his law, and we immediately begin to think, "I may not be perfect, but I am certainly a cut above other people." What is this thinking if not pharisaic—the detestable idea that God grades on a curve and that we can somehow work our way into his favor. The temptation religious people face is always to find comfort in our performance of the law, rather than in reliance on Jesus. "Just tell me how I should live, Jesus, so I can be pleasing to you. Then I'll clean up my act." We want security in our own lifestyle rather than in him.

Jesus Christ has only one answer for people in every age: The Son of Man is Lord of the Sabbath. He is, in fact, the very Sabbath rest for God's people. For in his Word and sacraments, he is present to give us his peace, solace, comfort, and quiet joy in the complete forgiveness of sins. He has gained our approval before God by his death and resurrection. We couldn't do it. He did. We are at peace with God—at rest—because of Jesus, the Lord of the Sabbath.

Lord, as you awaken us to delight in your praise, grant that we may know you, call on you, and praise you, for you have made us for yourself and our hearts are restless until they rest in you. Amen.

St. Augustine

53. Satan: The Deceiver Undone

And there was war in heaven. . . . The great dragon was hurled down—that ancient serpent called the devil, or Satan, who leads the whole world astray. He was hurled to the earth, and his angels with him. (Revelation 12:7,9)

You and I get used to evil. We are accustomed to living in a fallen world, so we take sin and all its consequences for granted. Like fish living in a foul, polluted river, we assume that evil is simply part and parcel of living in this world. But evil was never part of God's original creation. All was good and perfect, both among the people of earth and among the angels in heaven. But war broke out in heaven because Satan was not content to be a servant of God; he wanted to be like God himself. So he led a civil war among the angels.

All of this was the prelude to the fall of our first parents when the devil succeeded in luring first Eve and then Adam to follow him. Both ate of the forbidden fruit of Eden and in so doing brought sin into the world and death by sin. Thus in Adam all die. Death was the cruel hoax foisted upon God's perfect creation through the insurrection of the devil.

We must learn two things about Satan. The first is that the devil is a real and powerful enemy. He is mighty, though not almighty like God. The second is that the devil, thrown down to earth, is the sworn enemy of God and of the kingdom of God. The devil specializes in spoiling the creation of God. He seduces the faithful into false belief, despair, and other great shame and vice. Nothing delights the devil more than undermining God's kingdom, the church. That is why our Lord Jesus taught us to pray that our heavenly Father would not lead us into temptation, but deliver us from evil—or more precisely, the evil one.

We wrestle not against flesh and blood, it is true, but against the spiritual hosts of wickedness in heavenly places. Yet the cosmic battle has been won. Neither Satan, an angel gone horribly bad, nor his demonic hordes have any ultimate power to destroy. Now have come the salvation and the power of the kingdom of our God—and the authority of his Christ.

God's almighty power has gained the victory over Satan and his angels. God's victory came in an unexpected way. God punished his Son for the sins of all the world and crushed the power of Satan with a triumphant resurrection. Christ even descended into hell and returned in order to demonstrate the end of Satan's power.

By his cross and resurrection, Jesus Christ has undone all the power of the devil to destroy. Our Lord has demolished death, defeated the devil, and conquered all the forces of hell itself. In our Lord's precious Word and sacraments, we have our share in the victory yet to come. Satan is beaten down, and the kingdom of God advances against the kingdom of the devil. Already now in the forgiveness of our sins, we have, by faith, what we shall one day enjoy face-to-face: the resurrection of the body and life everlasting.

Let your holy angel be with me, that the wicked foe may have no power over me. Amen.

Martin Luther

54. Sheep without a Shepherd

When Jesus landed and saw a large crowd, he had compassion on them, because they were like sheep without a shepherd. So he began teaching them many things. (Mark 6:34)

Sheep without a shepherd are just an accident waiting to happen. In the wilderness when a sheep is separated from its shepherd, it's only a matter of time until you have dead meat. That's the way it was that day in the Galilean wilderness. Jesus took one look at the milling crowd, and that's what he saw—a people at risk. They were people dying of spiritual malnutrition, vulnerable and open to attack from stalking spiritual predators. His heart went out to them.

I wonder if our hearts go out to the people around us, as did the heart of Jesus. What happens when we take an honest look at the shame and corruption on every side in our world? Maybe it's time we take another look at the immorality and the idolatry running rampant all around us and see the emptiness, confusion, and loneliness that lie at the heart of it all. Maybe it's time we take another look at sinners and see them with the eyes of Jesus and have compassion for them. For they have no comfort, no nourishment or strength, no ultimate protection, no shelter or refuge. They have no shepherd. Yet all are in God's heart. He sent his Son to bleed and die that they all might be his own and live faithfully within his kingdom.

We too are sheep for whom the Good Shepherd laid down his life. Yet we are sinners all. The holy Christian church is not a museum of religious tradition or a display for rare moral acts. It is the body of Christ on earth, where the living gospel is preserved and proclaimed, where Christ's sacraments are administered for sinners. The church is not a cozy community club that provides us with the kinds of services we want. In it sinners are absolved in the name of Jesus and find the spiritual strength in Jesus to live for him.

Jesus Christ loves his sheep too much to give them what they want. Instead, he gives them what they need for this world and the next: the very bread of heaven, the Bread of Life. For he himself is the living Bread, which came down from heaven to bring life to the world. We need no spiritual junk food, you and I. We need the lasting food that endures to eternal life.

We need the Good Shepherd. For he and he alone has the words of eternal life. In his Holy Word, we find what we truly need—both God's solemn judgment against sin and the sweet promise of the forgiveness of all our sins in Jesus' name. He takes that forgiveness and joins it to his Word in Holy Baptism, and so makes it a bath of life for this dying world. He takes that forgiveness and joins it to his body and blood offered to us to eat and to drink under bread and wine. With his forgiveness comes life in all its fullness here and eternally with God in heaven

Almighty and eternal God, since you have brought back from the dead the great Shepherd of the sheep to call us into his flock by the Word, grant us your Holy Spirit so that we may hear the voice of the Good Shepherd and faithfully follow him who lives and reigns with you and the Holy Spirit, one God, now and forever. Amen.

Australian Anglican Alternative Collects, adapted

55. Shepherding the Flock

Keep watch over yourselves and all the flock of which the Holy Spirit has made you overseers. Be shepherds of the church of God, which he bought with his own blood. (Acts 20:28)

What you and I need today is encouragement and correction. It is for this very purpose that God has given pastors to his church. We benefit greatly from their care and keeping. The instructions St. Paul left behind for the leaders at Ephesus are as valid today as they were nearly two thousand years ago "Be shepherds of the church of God, which he bought with his own blood." We need faithful shepherds—shepherds who will not only guide us into the green pastures of God's rich grace, but shepherds who will also guard us from all harm.

Jesus, the Good Shepherd, laid down his life for every one of the sheep, purchasing each one with his own blood. He's the one who wants his sheep fed and nourished, guarded and protected. The Lord Jesus Christ ascended up on high that he might give gifts to his church on earth. So he gave some to be pastors and teachers, and he has charged them to do his work among us. They are to give full attention and unswerving devotion to Christ's ministry among us. That means teaching sound doctrine, not for its own sake, but because Christian doctrine is the teaching of Jesus. By this sound teaching, faithful Christians are encouraged, and erring Christians are corrected.

There are some who would say it doesn't matter what you teach or preach, just as long as people feel religious. But Jesus didn't come to make people happy.

He came instead to give them life with him, both now and to all eternity. Yet there is so much in our hearts that interferes with that life of Christ. Everything within our hearts and minds that stands in opposition to our God and to his kingdom must be rooted out and destroyed. That doesn't make us happy. Our sinful hearts find no joy in repentance. We think we can deal with sin on our own. But try as we might, we cannot. Jesus, our Good Shepherd, has intervened. He was made to be our sin instead of us, giving his life and shedding his blood that we might be forgiven.

In fact, Jesus himself speaks through the mouth of his called servants wherever his Word is rightly preached. Jesus speaks personally and specifically to forgive our sins when the pastor pronounces forgiveness in Jesus' name. Jesus himself gives his own body to eat and his blood to drink wherever his sacrament is administered faithfully. Jesus Christ feeds and nourishes his sheep using the voice and hands of the pastors he has sent. Christ works through them to touch our lives. Our pastors care for us in his name, by his command, and in his stead, so that we may remain ever faithful to God's Word and always fervent in his service to his eternal glory.

Lord of the Church, we humbly pray
For those who guide us in Thy way
And speak Thy holy Word.
With love divine their hearts inspire
And touch their lips with hallowed fire
And needful strength afford. Amen.

Edward Osler

56. The Silence of God

A Canaanite woman from that vicinity came to him, crying out, "Lord, Son of David, have mercy on me! My daughter is suffering terribly from demon-possession." Jesus did not answer a word. (Matthew 15:22,23)

The woman kept clamoring after Jesus; the disciples even urged Jesus to send the woman away. Yet her prayer was a confession of confident faith as well as a confession of despair. She cried out for deliverance from the pain and hopelessness in her life. We may be shocked to observe that "Jesus did not answer a word."

Doesn't it seem that way with us as well at times? At one time or another, we all come to the end of our rope. We all may find ourselves trapped in perilously tight spots with no solutions in sight. We have done all that we know how to do, and we turn to our Lord with hope and faith. From time to time, we meet the same response the Canaanite woman received: Jesus does not answer a word. What then? How do we handle the silence of God? Let this woman be a lesson to us.

Here was a woman who persisted in prayer. There are times we are tempted to give up. She kept praying. After all, Jesus didn't say no. He just didn't say anything. Here was a woman who knew how to cope with the silence of God. She believed and held fast to the Word of God. She clung to his promises, even when she was met with stony silence. The woman persisted, obstinately crying out, "Lord, Son of David, have mercy on me!" God's mercy was the only hope she had left in this world. At the same time, God's grace was all she needed. Jesus was moved by her faith, and his heart was open to hear her plea. Jesus healed her daughter.

We learn once again what it means to cling to his Word in the face of his silence. We learn once more what his love is all about. Though he is sometimes silent to our pleas, he is never inattentive to our needs. He allows us to be wounded so that we may learn to turn to him with faith and be healed by the miracle of his sufficient grace. He teaches us patience under affliction so that we may learn new dimensions of his love. So in the face of God's silence, we learn to pray without ceasing.

Every hurting soul and every burdened heart can come to him in the confidence of prayer. We cling to his gospel word, trusting in the abundance of his mercy and the riches of his grace, which he poured out once long ago upon his cross and offers us still in the gospel message and the sacraments.

Almighty God, whose Son, Jesus Christ, chose to suffer pain before going up to joy and crucifixion before entering into glory, mercifully grant that we, walking in the way of the cross, may find this path to be the way of life and peace; through Jesus Christ, your Son, our Lord, who lives and reigns with you and the Holy Spirit, one God, now and forever. Amen.

Collect for Holy Week

57. Strong Hands and Brave Hearts

Strengthen the feeble hands, steady the knees that give way; say to those with fearful hearts, "Be strong, do not fear; your God will come, he will come with vengeance; with divine retribution he will come to save you."
(Isaiah 35:3,4)

Knowing what we know about the promises of God, it would be good to leap right over all the unpleasantries of life and go for the fullness of his promise, which still lies in the future. It would be nice if we didn't have to wait for the complicated plot of our lives to unfold. It would be nice to skip over all of that and go right to the final chapter and the joys waiting us on the last page of eternity.

But that's not the way it works in the real world. We know that sometimes real life is not very pleasant. The word of the Lord says, "Strengthen the feeble hands, steady the knees that give way. . . ." That's us, isn't it? Feeble hands and weak knees. We lose our courage in this world, especially when the winds of adversity blow long and hard. If you've ever faced chronic pain or illness, you understand. If you've ever dealt with the emotional pain of loneliness or the heartache of disappointment or the aching loss of someone you love, you know that hands become feeble at times and knees get pretty wobbly. Then there's fear. We fear for someone else or fear for ourselves—fear for life and health or fear of the unknown. Whatever the kind of fear, it leaves the heart in a vise and the stomach tied in knots. Isaiah the prophet speaks directly to the likes of us today. He says, "Be strong, do not fear; your God will come."

Now, talk is cheap. Anybody can tell us to be strong and not to fear. But this is not just advice on how to be a more successful person. This is the Word of God. This

113

is the voice of the Lord, the God of the covenant, speaking through the mouth of his prophet. Isaiah, in the strength and power of the Holy Spirit, looked far into the future, grabbed a fistful of the promises of God, and thrust them right into the fearful hearts of the people of Judah. "Your God will come," he promised. And come he did, in Jesus Christ, to save. With retribution and with vengeance, Isaiah prophesied. In Jesus' death on the cross, God the Lord wreaked havoc on death and the devil. By Jesus' sacrificial death and triumphant resurrection, he broke the stranglehold of death and brought life and immortality to light through the gospel. We know that he will come again to awaken all his faithful from their graves and grant them the crown of life everlasting.

"Be strong, do not fear," for God comes to you now to bear your heartache and your fear—to wrap his arms around you. In his Word and sacraments, he gives you comfort and peace; he strengthens you in your weakness and quiets you with his gracious presence. In the gospel you have the strength and courage you need right now and to all eternity!

Almighty God, since you know that we are set in the midst of so many and great dangers that we cannot stand upright because of the frailty of our nature, grant us strength and protection to support us in all dangers and carry us through all temptations, through your Son, Jesus Christ our Lord. Amen.

Australian Anglican Alternative Collects, adapted

58. This Great Mystery

**This is a profound mystery—but I am talking about
Christ and the church. (Ephesians 5:32)**

Over the years we all have gathered with family or
friends to celebrate wedding days. We have delighted
in the ceremony, the feasting, and the abundant joy. It
is a day to capture on film and to be treasured in albums
and in memory. Yet as much as brides in their lovely bridal
gowns resemble Cinderella and grooms take the part of
Prince Charming, a wedding is no fairy tale. In truth,
it is the marriage, not the wedding glitter, that counts.

Marriage cannot be built solely on glamorous fables
of romantic love and the frailties of human promises.
Rather, marriage founded on Jesus Christ is designed
by God himself for the care and keeping of his children.
He has promised to bless therein all who serve him in
love and in faith. It is holy ground, for within the great
mystery of marriage, God gives us a glimpse of the very
union of Christ and his own bride, the church. The
mystery is that the union of earthly men and women
should mirror the relationship of Christ and his church.
Earthly husbands and wives—in their lives, in their
very bodies—should practice the very love, honor, and
unity of Jesus Christ and his holy bride, the church.

The greatest love story of all time tells us how the
Son of God set aside all his heavenly glory to come
among us and take on human flesh to woo and win for
himself a people of his own choosing. Worse than
Cinderella in her rags, we sinners are clothed in rebellion
and sin. Yet even that could not extinguish the love of
the heavenly groom for his beloved. He loves the church

115

and gave himself up for her. He cleansed her in his baptismal washing so that he might present the church to himself in splendor—a bride, holy, pure, and radiant with the bridegroom's love.

Each woman assumes the role and image of Christ's bride each day she lives as a loving wife to her husband. Each husband takes on the role and image of Christ as he loves his wife as his own body and nourishes and cherishes her as Christ does the church. Christian marriage is built on the solid foundation of God's sure Word and love, wrapped up in his cross and death for us and our salvation. No greater love could bind us. No greater love could sustain, strengthen, and comfort us. What a bond of love husbands and wives have in Christ! His love remains forever sure, this day and all our days, a legacy to pass along to our children and their children after them.

The Church's one foundation Is Jesus Christ, her Lord. She is his new creation by water and the Word. From heaven he came and sought her to be his holy bride. With his own blood he bought her, and for her life he died. Help us, Lord Jesus, to pattern our love for one another after your great love for us. Amen.

Samuel J. Stone, adapted

59. Those Who Trespass against Us

Then the master called the servant in. "You wicked servant," he said, "I canceled all that debt of yours because you begged me to. Shouldn't you have had mercy on your fellow servant just as I had on you?"
(Matthew 18:32,33)

There's something about the parable of the unforgiving servant that leaves us with a chill. When Jesus tells us how the royal master turned his unforgiving servant over to the jailers for torture, he turns to us, looks us right in the eye, and lays it on the line. He said, "This is how my heavenly Father will treat each of you unless you forgive your brother from your heart" (Matthew 18:35).

Now the truth is, forgiveness doesn't come naturally for any of us. We learn from little on that there's only one way to handle pain. If somebody kicks you, you kick them back. If somebody calls you names, you call them names. Christians, of course, aren't supposed to act that way. But, in the real world, when push comes to shove, you'd better be sure you shove the hardest. It's the law of the jungle. That law prevails on inner-city streets, on suburban playgrounds, in corporate boardrooms, and around kitchen tables. Retaliation is the name of the game, sadly, even among Christians. As we grow older and more sophisticated, we hide our feelings and channel our anger. We no longer fight back; instead, we clam up and do a silent burn.

We carry a big, imaginary garbage bag with us. Every time somebody hurts us, whenever we suffer wrongs or injuries, we store them in that garbage bag. That bag comes in handy, after all. We open it up and rummage through the garbage whenever we're hurt. And sure enough, we come up with some other hurt that person caused us a long time ago. We hang on to all those hurts simply to nurse our anger at people and then get back at them for all the dirt they've done to us. We savor our bitterness.

But you don't have to carry garbage around anymore. You can bury the hurts and wrongs that fester away in bitterness and hatred. Jesus Christ has another way of handling hurt and pain—not with retaliation but with forgiveness, not with anger but with love. He died not just for you but even for those who hurt you and hurt you deeply. All of your pain was his on his cross. All of your hurt was his in his suffering. All of your injuries were his in his death. He took it all with him into his death and disposed of it once and for all in his tomb. "I forgive you," he says. Yet as we rejoice in Christ's forgiveness, we sometimes refuse to forgive other people. But Christ gives new power to forgive from the heart. He first cleanses our hearts by his precious gospel and then gives us the power to forgive. In Jesus Christ your hearts are free to love as he has loved and to forgive as he has forgiven! Therefore we pray, "Our Father in heaven, forgive us our sins, as we forgive those who sin against us." When we understand and believe Christ's forgiveness, we will forgive others for his sake.

O Lord and Father, to whom alone those in great debt can come with hope of mercy, have mercy on us, who have nothing with which to repay you. Forgive us all our sins, and make us merciful to others for the sake of Jesus Christ our Lord. Amen.

Lancelot Andrewes

60. Tribulation and Healing

In this world you will have trouble. But take heart! I have overcome the world. (John 16:33)

We live in a world of stress and turmoil. We live in a world where jammed calendars and frazzled nerves are badges of honor, demonstrating to everyone that we're hard workers and go-getters. Our world surrounds us with information available at our fingertips, and our technology of choice bombards us with constant stimulation. Yet we live increasingly isolated lives, more alone than ever before. This is a world out of touch with people and, most tragically of all, out of touch with God. Despite all that is good, we live in a sick world. A world that is sick at heart.

Yet there is hope in this sin-sick world. In the darkness Light has dawned. Into the death of this world, Life has come to heal the sick: that's you and me. We are sick, whether we feel it or not. Some of us face an empty chair at the table and a gaping hole in our hearts because someone we love has died. Others wait for medical reports with uncertain outcomes. Still others are heartsick with worry over others—an abusive spouse, a rebellious child, a hurting friend. In this world of ours, it seems there is nothing we can do except grin and bear it. After a while our grins get a bit plastic, for we discover that we can't rebuild the rubble of a broken heart with sheer personal determination.

But the Son of God cries out in victory from his cross, "I have overcome the world." And he means exactly what he says. No matter what your fear, your guilt, or your private pain, he came to heal. To people who have lost all hope, he says, "Take heart!" Anybody can say, "Have a nice day," but only Jesus Christ, the Son of God, can bring real hope. Anybody can say, "Cheer up," but only Jesus Christ can take our pain away. He can because he bore it all long ago in his own body on his cross. He has taken all our sin and grief on himself and destroyed it all in his death and resurrection.

Jesus Christ, only Son of the Father, comes into this sick and weary world of ours. Perhaps he comes in ways we take for granted, but he does indeed come. When his Word is proclaimed, he stands in our midst. When we receive the bread and wine of the Holy Supper, we also receive the very body and blood given and shed for us for the forgiveness of sins. When his called servants stand before his people and say, "I forgive you all your sins," he forgives them. In this harried, troubled world, through Word and sacraments, he heals us with his love and his forgiveness.

In the depths of my pain, Lord Jesus, come. Surround me with your love, and lift me from dark depression. When I am weary, lift my spirit and give me hope with your simple words, "Take heart! I have overcome the world." Because you love me and promise never to leave me, I come boldly with my humble prayer. Amen.

Paul Gerhardt, adapted

61. The Trinity at Work

May the grace of the Lord Jesus Christ, and the love of God, and the fellowship of the Holy Spirit be with you all. (2 Corinthians 13:14)

The Holy Trinity is ceaselessly, tirelessly at work in his holy church, bestowing wonderful gifts to all his own. We can see that clearly in the familiar blessing of the text. The first thing that strikes us about the benediction is the boldness of it. It's not a pious hope or vague wish, as if the apostle were hoping that these things would come to pass. These words actually confer what they describe. Wherever God puts his name, there he is present to bless. The glorious realities of grace, love, and fellowship are the work of the Holy Trinity, freely bestowed upon his children on the basis of his promise. It is his bold promise with no strings attached.

In this blessing we see the Holy Trinity at work, cohesively as one God, and yet specifically and uniquely, as three separate persons. That's why we can neither confess the Holy Trinity nor worship him apart from the grace of our Lord Jesus Christ, God's Son. That's exactly what we receive from the Son—his grace and undeserved love. It is the free gift of the Father's love, filtered through the agony and bloody sweat of the cross. It is the Father's love brought home and bestowed upon us poor miserable sinners at the expense of the holy, innocent, bitter sufferings and death of his beloved Son, Jesus Christ.

And thank God we do know that grace of Jesus Christ. We know it not as we know the alphabet or the multiplication tables, but as we know life itself. We absolutely cling to that grace; we live by that grace.

The grace of the Lord Jesus Christ is our personal, individual gift from the Holy Trinity, with love.

But without the Holy Spirit we would know nothing. It is the Holy Spirit who dispenses all that originates within the loving heart of the Father, earned by the cross and resurrection of his Son. God's Word and the sacraments are the actual channels by which God the Holy Spirit delivers the goods. The Word and sacraments are tangible links with God. This is the route by which eternity breaks into time. In God the Holy Spirit, there is a link between God in heaven and his holy people in this world, made holy by his grace.

God's very Word, his presence, his blessing, and his gifts cannot be comprehended. We bless him; we glorify him. We bless one God in our praise of three persons. And in the three persons, we worship and glorify one God, now and forever. We continually worship and honor one Holy Trinity with the words of our lips, the meditation of our hearts, and the service of our very bodies—to the Father, through the Son, in the power of the Holy Spirit.

Bless us, God the Father, you that have created us. Bless us, God the Son, you that have set us free. Bless us, God the Holy Spirit, you that have made us holy. O blessed Trinity, keep us in body, soul, and spirit to life eternal. Amen.

Weimarischer Gesangbuch, 1873

62. True Wisdom

The fear of the LORD is the beginning of wisdom, and the knowledge of the Holy One is understanding. (Proverbs 9:10)

Whether we are intellectuals or not, we all in our own way want answers about this world. What happens to those who have climbed on the merry-go-round of casual sex and found it not so merry? How about those who have climbed on the bandwagon of success and achievement, believing its promise of a life of luxury and personal fulfillment? They want to know why their work has become all-consuming, a vacuum sucking the life out of them. What about those with broken relationships, memories of past sins, and lives aching with guilt? They want to know what to do with the broken pieces of their lives.

We need answers for our own pain as well. We'd like to know what to do when our hearts cry out for the love of God but we feel nothing but emptiness inside. We'd like to know what to do when the burden of life seems heavy and the yoke of our faith seems hard to bear. Each of us asks, "Where is God when I need him? How can I be sure he is real? How can I know I'm forgiven, that I'm loved, and that I'm his?" We'd really like to know. Then there are the times we pray and seem to get no answer—when no matter how hard we beat on heaven's door, there seems to be no one home. We'd like to know, "Where in the world is God?"

In the midst of all this overwhelming need comes this simple Word from God, "The fear of the LORD is the beginning of wisdom." To fear the Lord is to believe in him. The great search of human beings for knowledge begins and ends in Jesus Christ. He is the wisdom of God. He came to suffer and to die. But in his death he released us from all the pain and misery of this world of ours. It was our death he died, and it is his life we live. When you know him by faith, you know God. The knowledge of the Holy One is understanding.

There's really nothing more important in this world than to know Christ—the fellowship of his suffering and the power of his resurrection. That's what makes sense of this world, its pain and agony. Jesus invites us to take up our cross and follow him. Whatever cross we bear in life, we follow the great cross bearer. He carried his cross to Calvary and then hung on the cross in our place. As we carry our crosses, he comes to us as he always has in the words of the gospel, in the washing of water by the Spirit, and in the bread and wine. He continues coming to us again and again with precisely what we need—the message of his unconditional and unlimited love. His message is direct and powerful, "Fear not, for I have redeemed you; I have summoned you by name; you are mine" (Isaiah 43:1). And that's all we will ever really need to know in this life or the next.

O Lord, since you never fail to help and guide those whom you bring up in your fear and love, give us continual fear and love for your holy name, through your Son, Jesus Christ our Lord, who lives and reigns with you and the Holy Spirit, one God, now and forever. Amen.

Australian Anglican Alternative Collects, adapted

63. 20/20 Vision

Why do you look at the speck of sawdust in your brother's eye and pay no attention to the plank in your own eye? How can you say to your brother, "Let me take the speck out of your eye," when all the time there is a plank in your own eye? (Matthew 7:3,4)

We have 20/20 vision when it comes to seeing specks in the eyes of others, but we somehow miss the planks in our own eyes. We can detect anger and bitterness a mile away in those we work with, but when we ourselves are angry, suddenly it is justified anger. We were hurt, we were wronged, or it was the other person's fault. We know pride and arrogance when we see it in others, but somehow the person we see in the mirror is not proud or arrogant. He or she is self-confident, assertive, or a self-starter. When it comes to our own sin, we have a blind spot.

Our eyes are not particularly well-suited for seeing things as they really are. We live in a world of darkness, and we are blinded by our own sin. We deplore the immorality and darkness of our reckless world, which seems to be drowning in a cesspool of greed, lust, and flagrant immorality. Yet we find it difficult to admit that we ourselves stand condemned by the same law with which we condemn our sinful world.

Mercifully, in this world of darkness, a light shines. It is the light of the sure Word of God. Jesus teaches, "I am the light of the world. Whoever follows me will never walk in darkness, but will have the light of life" (John 8:12). The sure Word of God sheds light into this dark and confusing world of sin. But more than that, the very same Word of God brings light to those of us who live in the darkness and walk in the blindness of our sin. For the cross of Christ is not just a fact of ancient history. His saving work is not just an idea or a concept from long ago. The forgiveness of our sin that Jesus achieved for all the world on the cross comes to us here and now. When we hear the gospel, God applies that forgiveness to us. "If we claim to be without sin, we deceive ourselves and the truth is not in us," we read in the first letter of St. John. "If we confess our sins, he is faithful and just and will forgive our sins and purify us from all unrighteousness" (1 John 1:8,9).

And that's exactly what happens in the liturgy. We confess our sins, and the pastor speaks the Word of God to forgive those sins: as a called and ordained servant of the Word, every pastor speaks for Jesus and forgives you all your sins in the name of the Father and of the Son and of the Holy Spirit. The absolution is the forgiveness of Jesus himself, which means light for our darkness and sight for our blindness. Already here in the very shadow of death, we bask in the sunshine of his love and walk in the brightness of his light, which has no end.

Look down, O Lord, from your heavenly throne; illuminate the darkness of this night with your celestial brightness; and from the children of light, banish the deeds of darkness, through Jesus Christ our Lord. Amen.

Gelasian

64. The Waiting Father

So he got up and went to his father. But while he was still a long way off, his father saw him and was filled with compassion for him; he ran to his son, threw his arms around him and kissed him. (Luke 15:20)

It's no secret that fatherhood is in crisis in our society today. We see an increasing number of addicted fathers, abusive fathers, and absent fathers. Tragically, we see fewer and fewer "real" fathers—men in whom initiative and strength are combined with tenderness and love for their children. It is, without a doubt, a real crisis in family life. But I would suggest to you that there is a deeper crisis underlying the breakup of the family in our land. It is what I call the "love famine."

How can children grow up to become loving adults if they have never known how to love and to be loved? How can mothers invest their lives in the nurturing of their children if they have no understanding of what it means to be a child of their heavenly Father? How can a man be a responsible father to his children without first knowing what it means to be a son—a son of the heavenly Father? In fact, how can any one of us, man or woman, married or single, adult or child, really learn to love if we never get the first lesson—the love of God the Father in heaven?

The parable of the prodigal son is a beautiful story, as Jesus told it. But what's even more beautiful is that it's not just a story; it has a profound application in reality. We learn that no matter how far you and I may have wandered away from our home, there's always a place for us in the Father's house. No matter how shamefully we have lived and no matter how disgusted we have been with ourselves, still our heavenly Father waits and watches, eager to welcome us in his loving embrace. He is not interested in punishing us for our failures. For he made his own Son to be sin for us so that we might have his own perfection and holiness. He gave up his own perfect Son to the shame of the cross, where he endured the just penalty for our sin. God's Son took all the misery of our sin and death and nailed it to his cross so that he might welcome us into life in all its fullness already here and now.

That's how we learn what love is all about. At the foot of the cross, there is room for every prodigal son and daughter eager for healing. There is no love famine here, because we have a waiting Father, filled with compassion for each of us. In every gospel absolution, in every Holy Supper eaten, you will hear the Word of the Father as he enfolds you in his loving embrace. "Welcome home, my child!" he says.

Father, how often I have sinned against you and found pleasure in the stench of sin. Forgive me, heavenly Father. Remove from me the foul garment of sin, and exchange it for the pure garment of forgiveness in your Son, Jesus. Then Lord help me love others as I am loved by you. Amen.

Unknown

65. We Are the Lord's

If we live, we live to the Lord; and if we die, we die to the Lord. So, whether we live or die, we belong to the Lord. For this very reason, Christ died and returned to life so that he might be the Lord of both the dead and the living. (Romans 14:8,9)

Christianity is a matter of life and death and life again. In Jesus Christ, we are given the gift to live life to the full and then to lay life down again in confidence and hope that we will live again. The creed each Christian confesses repeatedly and confidently in baptismal faith puts it pointedly and clearly: I believe in the resurrection of the body and the life everlasting.

Holy Scripture declares that there is a time to live and a time to die. For some of the saints, the time to die has come and gone. For the rest of us, the saints on earth, that chapter of our lives has yet to be written. We are reminded that our lives on this earth will be eclipsed by eternity. The best is yet to come. For Christ not only died, he came to life again so that he might be Lord both of the dead and of the living. Everyone baptized into Christ Jesus is baptized into his death and resurrection. We can be confident that because we have shared in his death, we shall also share in his resurrection. That eternal truth and promise gives the Christian certainty in uncertain times.

On the Last Day, every grave will be opened, and those who have died in Christ will be raised to share in his glory. In their flesh they shall behold him, and their eyes shall see him. In his cross and death Christ has destroyed death. By his rising to life again, he has broken the bonds of the grave and defeated death and hell.

129

Each of the saints who have fallen asleep in Christ will be brought with him on the day when he returns to judge the living and the dead.

Someone once said that the church is the only organization that does not disenfranchise its members because they happen to be dead. Christ is Lord both of the dead and of the living. By faith we have come to know that he is the very life of all who trust in him, whether here on earth or there in heaven. All baptized believers are at one in him.

Christianity is the faith by which we live and in which we shall die and then be raised. This is the faith that sustains us in our brightest days and our darkest nights. This is the faith worked in us by the Holy Spirit through the gospel in Word and sacraments. God cleanses us by the water and the Word so that we live before God in righteousness and purity now and forever.

O Lord, the first and the last, the beginning and the end, as you were with us in birth, be with us through life, be with us in death and because your mercy will not leave us then, grant that we do not die without hope, but rise to life forever with you and in you, for you live and reign in the glory of the eternal Trinity, one God, now and forever. Amen.

Cambridge Bede Book

66. When Life Caves In

The woman came and knelt before him. "Lord, help me!" she said. He replied, "It is not right to take the children's bread and toss it to their dogs." "Yes, Lord," she said, "but even the dogs eat the crumbs that fall from their masters' table." Then Jesus answered, "Woman, you have great faith! Your request is granted." And her daughter was healed from that very hour. (Matthew 15:25-28)

We come to Jesus exactly as this woman did. "*Kyrie Eleison,*" we cry. "Lord, have mercy." What else can you say when life caves in? What else can you say when your plans go up in smoke, when trusted friends turn their backs on you, or when each day seems like a minefield waiting to blow up in your face if you trip? "Kyrie Eleison—Lord, have mercy." What else can you say when danger and uncertainty seem to lurk around every corner? "Kyrie Eleison."

We learn a lot from this woman and that little prayer of hers. She came with no fancy prayer, no fine words, no impressive credentials. She came with nothing but her desperation and her faith. She laid it all out there in front of Jesus, with the very simple, yet utterly profound, words, "Lord, Son of David, have mercy on me." What we learn is that the greatest prayers are offered out of emptiness. There was nothing she could do anymore. There was no one to turn to except Jesus. She knew who Jesus was, and she came to him in simple faith, knelt before him in worship, and laid her heart bare to him. "Lord, help me," she said. Just that. Nothing more. You can't get much more direct.

Yet Jesus seemed almost callous in his response, "It is not right to take the children's bread," he said, "and toss it to their dogs." The very idea of comparing her to a dog! We would have been offended, but not this woman. It didn't matter to her that she was not an Israelite. She did not care that she didn't belong to the household by birth. She did belong to the household by faith, and that made all the difference in the world. "Yes, Lord," she said, "but even the dogs eat the crumbs that fall from their masters' table." When refused bread, she was satisfied with the crumbs.

Like this woman we too come before God with empty hands. We don't qualify for anything from God on the basis of our pedigree or our track record. Yet Jesus was sent not just for the lost sheep of the house of Israel but for the entire world. His hours of bitter agony on the cross, his death and resurrection earned forgiveness for all. There is no sin so vile, there is no heart so hardened, there is no life so broken that God cannot bring his forgiveness and healing. So, like this woman, we bring our kyries too. "Lord, have mercy" we cry. And God meets us in his Word and sacraments, bringing the very presence of Christ and his power and strength. He has mercy and forgives. In his forgiveness we find courage, life, hope, and peace, both now and forever.

> To you, omniscient Lord of all,
> With grief and shame I humbly call;
> I see my sins against you, Lord,
> The sins of thought, of deed and word.
> They press me so sore;
> To you I flee,
> O God, be merciful to me! Amen.

Magnus B. Landstad

67. When Others Sin against Us

If your brother sins against you, go and show him his fault, just between the two of you. If he listens to you, you have won your brother over. (Matthew 18:15)

We all know what it's like when someone sins against us, and we're pretty sure we know how to handle the situation. If someone sins against us, we just tell them to buzz off. We either tell them off first and then tell them to get lost, or we just tell them to get lost right off the bat. That's a routine way of dealing with sin—not dealing with it. We just turn our backs on those who sin against us, acting as though that sin were not our problem. Jesus teaches us otherwise. He teaches us that the brother who has sinned against us IS our problem. He has robbed us of his brotherhood by his sin, and it's up to us to restore the relationship. That's why our brother's sin is a reason to go to him to win him back, not to write him off.

We are to go to our brother and tell him his fault, just between the two of us. Often if we tell anyone, it's surely not the one who has sinned against us. We go and talk to somebody else who will give us some sympathy—somebody who will agree with us, somebody who will help us bad-mouth our brother and help us destroy his reputation. Instead of going to those who have hurt us by their sins against us, we may have nursed our wounds and carried a grudge. There are far too many casualties in the wars we wage against those who have sinned against us. How many of us fail to heed the words of Jesus?

Jesus has a different word for us, a word not of condemnation nor retaliation, but a word of forgiveness.

133

That's how God deals with sin, you see. He doesn't sweep sin under the rug, nor does he harbor grudges in his heart. He confronts us with our sin in his holy law. He brings our sin out into the open so that we may repent and be saved. He took our sins with him and nailed them up on his cross. He took them all with him into his death, buried them in his tomb, and left them there when he emerged the victor in his glorious resurrection from the dead.

It is a wonderful miracle that by Christ's command and with his authority, one human being may announce to another human being the entire forgiveness of all his sins in Jesus' name—no more pretense, bitterness, or grudges. For God's sake tell your brother his fault. If that person speaks his sorrow over his sin and says, "Please forgive me," forgive that person from the heart, just as God has forgiven you in Christ. The best part is that when you have forgiven that person in the name of Jesus Christ, you have gained a brother!

God of love, through your only Son, you have given us a new commandment: that we should love one another as you love us, the unworthy and wandering. Give to us a mind ready to forget past ill will, a pure conscience, and a heart to love and forgive our brothers and sisters, through your Son, Jesus Christ our Lord. Amen.

St. Cyril

68. When Storms Arise

A furious squall came up, and the waves broke over the boat, so that it was nearly swamped. Jesus was in the stern, sleeping on a cushion. The disciples woke him and said to him, "Teacher, don't you care?"
(Mark 4:37,38)

It looked as if Jesus didn't care. There they were in trouble, with the ship about to go down, and he seemed oblivious to the storm. There they were about to drown, and Jesus was asleep, of all things, in the midst of their distress. They shook him awake with an urgent question, "Teacher, don't you care if we drown?" Some of us have felt that way in our lives too. At times we may have liked to shake Jesus by the shoulders, grab his attention, and ask, "Can't you see my situation? Aren't you going to do something about it?" When storms arise most of us react very much like the disciples and ask whether Jesus really cares.

Of course, he cared very much for his disciples, and he didn't want them to drown. He cared so much that he stood up in the boat and put a stop to the roaring winds and the turbulent waves. His word brought a great calm on the sea. That's what we all need when storms arise— great calm, a quiet peace, a silencing of all fear and turmoil.

We are all guilty, each in a different way, of the same sin as the disciples. In times of trouble, we have smallness of faith and distrust the Father's will. We lack confidence that God will see us through. What Jesus asked his disciples that night on the sea of Galilee, he could just as well ask us, "Why are you so afraid? Do you still have no faith?" It's not that we lose our faith every time we mistrust God's goodness. It's just that our faith is so pitifully weak that when storms arise we cannot see things as they really are. Jesus teaches us that things aren't the way they appear in this world. As the wind whipped the waves over the sides of the boat, it appeared as though the disciples would die and Jesus didn't care. Yet the power and the love of the Lord Jesus were just as real when he was asleep in the stern as when he rebuked the storm. It's just that his disciples couldn't see it. They were called upon to believe what they could not see so they would not be overtaken by fear.

The Bible says that when we are faithless, Christ remains faithful. His Word is stronger than our doubt. His Word brings peace in the very midst of distress to calm hearts that are battered and bruised by sin or weak with heartache. He loves us no matter how fierce the wind or high the waves. He demonstrated that love for us on the cross. With his own blood, he made payment in full for our sins. There is peace between God and man, because Christ himself is our peace. That peace is yours, no matter what storms may rage around you. His love and forgiveness is guaranteed to you in his Holy Word. Come what may, though lightnings flash and thunders crash, Jesus never fails his own. Secure in his redeeming love, we may live always in his perfect peace, even when storms arise.

Lord, help of the helpless, hope of those past hope, rescuer of the storm-tossed, harbor of the voyagers, healer of the sick, we ask you to assure us of your deep love for us all. When we fret and worry, turn us to your Word for comfort. Bestow on us your peace and love through Jesus Christ, our Savior. Amen.

St. Basil, adapted

69. Your Ticket to Heaven

Then the mother of Zebedee's sons came to Jesus with her sons and, kneeling down, asked a favor of him. "What is it you want?" he asked. She said, "Grant that one of these two sons of mine may sit at your right and the other at your left in your kingdom." "You don't know what you are asking," Jesus said to them. "Can you drink the cup I am going to drink?" "We can," they answered. (Matthew 20:20-22)

Every mother wants the best for her children. Though the other disciples weren't too happy with what looked like a display of ambition, we understand what led Mrs. Zebedee to ask such a thing of Jesus. She wanted Jesus to grant seats of honor to her sons.

That particular prize came with a high price tag. "You don't know what you are asking," Jesus said. "Can you drink the cup I am going to drink?" We know the cup he was talking about. He mentioned it again the night before his execution on the cross, "Father, if it is possible, may this cup be taken from me. Yet not as I will, but as you will" (Matthew 26:39). He was talking about his death, of course. But more than that, the cup was the Father's wrath against the sins of all humanity. In fact, it was the cup of death he was about to drink. Here he turns to this well-meaning mother and her two fine strapping boys just on the threshold of manhood and says, "Can you drink the cup I am going to drink?"

James and John answered, "We can." They didn't know what they were saying. As zealous and sincere as they were, they had no idea what the kingdom of Jesus involved. This mother wanted seats of honor for her sons, one on either side of Jesus. Jesus had something else in mind. Matthew 27:38 records that after the soldiers nailed Jesus to his cross, "Two robbers were crucified with him, one on his right and one on his left." That hill called Calvary was the throne room of the kingdom of God, you see. His crown was of thorns, and his throne was a cross. His triumph was in death.

This is the sum total of the kingdom of God. In fact, it is your ticket to heaven—Jesus and his cross. We shall know his victory in the kingdom yet to come. But here, in the meantime, we share his woe. The seats of honor in his kingdom are bestowed by the Father, but they are often seats of pain in this world. It is in the bearing of our crosses that we drink the cup of Jesus. We never can earn our salvation by what we suffer. Rather, this is the way we taste and see that the Lord is good.

We discover that when we're down and out, we sense the love of God most clearly. The psalmist writes, "Though the LORD is on high, he looks upon the lowly, but the proud he knows from afar" (Psalm 138:6). We drink from his cup when we suffer. But Jesus does not leave the cup bitter. He works even in our suffering to bring us perseverance, character, and hope (Romans 5:1-5). As we suffer he works all things to our advantage until he is ready for us to take the last sweet swallow of his cup and to give us life and joy forever in heaven. First the cross, and then the crown.

Grant, Lord, that I may glory only in the cross of our Lord Jesus Christ, through which the world has been crucified to me and I to the world. Amen.

Based on Galatians 6:14

70. Why Run on Empty?

A man can do nothing better than to eat and drink and find satisfaction in his work. This too, I see, is from the hand of God, for without him, who can eat or find enjoyment? (Ecclesiastes 2:24,25)

God makes no bones about it; when you play footsie with the ungodliness of the world, you're in spiritual danger. I believe that is why he gave us the book of Ecclesiastes—so that God's people in every age might take stock of things. It serves as a flashing, yellow caution light for everyone caught in the traffic jam of life in our confusing world today. It warns us to be careful that the cravings of the sinful nature, the lust of the eyes, and the pride of life do not take over for the things of God and his kingdom.

God tells us that there are only two kinds of people in the world: those who know and trust in him and those who don't—those whose lives are wrapped up in him and those who are wrapped up in themselves; those who find their joy and fulfillment in him and those who are still sifting through the rubble of this world, trying to piece together a life as best they can.

We need to learn this secret: "Godliness with contentment is great gain" (1 Timothy 6:6). That is, be content with what you have. Throw yourself into the life God has given you. Be the best husband you can be to your wife. Be the best wife, the best father or mother, the best son or daughter you can be. Be who God made you to be. God has placed you where you are with the unique gifts he has given you. God himself has given you a vocation in the very place you live and work.

No matter what you do each day, no matter what your job title, you are in partnership with God the

Father to care for his creation. Just imagine! You are his instrument in that enterprise. Through the work you do every day, God is busy supplying the daily bread of your neighbors. So quit looking somewhere else for fulfillment. Fulfillment and joy are right under your nose. "A man can do nothing better than to eat and drink and find satisfaction in his work. This too . . . is from the hand of God."

There once was a man who found perfect fulfillment in his work. His work, he said, was to do the will of the Father. His name is Jesus, and the work he did, he did for you. He laid down his life in death to bring you life. Not just any life, mind you, but life with God in all its fullness, already now and for all eternity. That life is here for you today in the gospel and sacraments Christ has given to his church. You no longer need to run on empty, breathless from the never-ending treadmill and rat race of life. In the forgiveness of your sins, you have a new beginning, a fresh start, right here and right now.

So let it begin today. Quit looking around for more and better. Be content with what God has given you richly and abundantly without any merit or worthiness in you. Count your blessings this day, and rejoice in your work. Then be thankful and find your joy in God.

Give me a faithful heart, likeness to thee,
That each departing day henceforth may see
Some work of love begun, some deed of kindness done,
Some wand'rer sought and won, something for thee. Amen.

Sylvanus D. Phelps

Index to Scripture References

Topical Reference by Chapter

Affliction

Why might God allow suffering to enter our lives? 7, 16, 23, 56

What does it mean to bear our crosses? 12, 16, 18, 51, 62

How can we receive the good gifts of God in the midst of suffering? 30, 57, 62

Why do bad things happen to good people? 2, 19

How does God console us in our pain? 13, 45, 60

Anxiety

How can we find courage for our fears? 24, 57, 68

How would God have us deal with the anxious moments in our lives? 6, 24

Do we have anything to fear at the time of judgment? 29, 65

How does God bring hope and healing to lives filled with turmoil? 32, 43, 60

Why does Jesus condemn our worry? 42

Baptism

How does God make us his own through Baptism? 35

What does it mean to "put on Christ"? 4

What does it mean to be "born again"? 8

Confession of Sin

How does confession of sin allow for our healing? 41

Why do we need God's courage to confess our sin? 40

What happens when we confess our sin before God? 25, 48

Death

Why can the Christian be confident and consoled at the time of death? 65, 69

How can we be holy in such an unholy world? 10

Do we exhibit godliness and holiness in our lives? 34

Kingdom of God

What is the kingdom of God like? 17, 41

When does God's kingdom come? 5

What are the fruits of the kingdom in our lives? 34

Living in, not of, this world

What does Jesus tell us about getting ahead in this world? 11

Why can we Christians remain confident as we move toward the 21st century? 5, 49

What should be most important in our lives? 1, 62, 70

How can a child of God live in a corrupt world? 10, 27, 33, 53

Marriage

Chastity is a little quaint for the 21st century, isn't it? 38

Why is marriage holy ground and a holy mystery? 58

Persecution

How can we remain confident when persecuted for our faith? 1

Possessions

How can our possessions begin to replace our God? 46

What can diminish our hunger for God? 26

How are we to live in a world where we have so much? 48

Prayer

What can we do if it seems that God isn't answering our prayers? 56

What does it mean to pray *Kyrie Eleison*? 66

How would our Lord have us pray? 44

What does Jesus Christ pray through us in our prayers? 31

Sin

The Touch of God

Worship

Wrath of God